Free Throw

Free Throw

7 Steps to Success at
the Free Throw Line

Dr. Tom Amberry
with Philip Reed

 HarperPerennial

A Division of HarperCollins*Publishers*

HarperCollins books may be purchased for educational, business, or sales promotional use. For information, please write to: Special Markets Department, HarperCollins*Publishers*, Inc., 10 East 53rd Street, New York, New York 10022.

FIRST EDITION

Library of Congress Cataloging-in-Publication Data

Amberry, Tom, 1922–
    Free throw : 7 steps to success at the free throw line / Tom Amberry with Philip Reed. —1st ed.
        p.   cm.
    ISBN 0-06-273434-2
    1. Free throw (Basketball)—I. Reed, Philip (Philip C.)—II. Title
GV888.2.A44   1996
796.323'2—dc20   96-15790

96 97 98 99 00 ❖/RRD 10 9 8 7 6 5 4 3 2 1

To my wife, Elon,
and our four boys,
Tim, Bill, Tom, and Robert

Contents

Contents

ACKNOWLEDGMENTS

First of all, I would like to thank all the basketball players and coaches I have had the pleasure of working with over the past few years while developing my shooting style and learning to teach it to others. The comments and suggestions I have received from so many different sources have been extremely helpful.

I owe special thanks to my friend Dr. Eric Rodney Hubbard for encouraging me to take up free throw shooting and starting me off on a wonderful adventure. I also would like to mention that many of my other doctor friends have shot with me and encouraged me in many ways.

Matt Wagner and David Fugate, at Waterside Productions, have my thanks for believing *Free Throw* was a good idea even before anything was on paper.

At HarperCollins Publishers, I would like to thank our editor, Robert Wilson, and all the other talented people who expertly guided the book through the process and made it such a wonderful experience.

Of all the coaches I've worked with, I owe the most to John Welch, assistant coach at Fresno State, who listened to me in the beginning and helped me get my start. Denyse and Chuck Campione were kind enough to give me my first clinic job. Many other coaches have been helpful and encouraging, such as Pat Douglass, Jerry Tarkanian, Jim Harrick, Bob Gottlieb, Seth Greenberg, and Howard Dewell.

I owe a special debt to Earl S. Strinden, at the University of North Dakota, for reading the book and putting it in the right hands. Another old friend, Gene Swartz, was also helpful. Coach Howard Lyons and James Ullrich, Esq., deserve special thanks for reading the book and giving me their expert feedback.

Many members of the print and electronic media have been very kind to me in person and even kinder in their articles and features. In particular I wish to thank Debbie Arrington, from the *Press Telegram*, for starting it all, and Mike and Jack Leonard for getting me on the air the first time.

I want to express my thanks to the staff of the Rossmoor Athletic Club, in Seal Beach, California, where I practice almost every morning, and to the basketball players who came to play but were occasionally displaced by TV cameras.

And finally, I want to thank my coauthor, Philip Reed, for helping me capture my ideas in words and for adding a few of his own, too.

PREFACE

The first time I heard of Dr. Tom Amberry was when I was sitting in a donut store having a cup of coffee. I was skimming a local newspaper, and my eyes fell on a story about a seventy-one-year-old retired podiatrist who had made 2,750 free throws in a row to enter *The Guinness Book of Records*.

I can remember reading the story several times thinking there had to be a mistake there somewhere. No one is capable of that level of perfection, especially at that age.

In the story Dr. Amberry was quoted as saying that his free throw shooting routine took six seconds and was like "auto hypnosis." Hypnosis has lurked around the edges of sports in an intriguing way for many years. But the idea of packaging it in six-second doses was new and very attractive to me.

For a long time I had been interested in repetitive action in sports. I was on the high school tennis team and knew how difficult it is on a crucial point to get your second serve in after hitting the first one long. On my college soccer team I was chosen to make the penalty kicks, which are even easier than sinking a free throw. It is considered virtually a guaranteed point in a game where scores are frequently 1–0. In one game, against a team we had never beaten, I put the ball over the cross bar of the goal. I can still see the ball whistling high and remember wondering why my body (or was it my mind?) had betrayed me in this crucial moment.

More recently, I became interested in golf. I soon discovered the problem that has faced all golfers trying to lower their score. As you get closer to the hole, your nerves get jumpier. Stories abound of missed putts from incredibly short distances down to 12 inches. I thought this retired podiatrist who sank 2,750 free throws in a row must know something that could be of great value to the millions of athletes around the world who are trying to put tennis balls in the service box, golf balls in cups, soccer balls in goals and, of course, basketballs in hoops.

I have long believed that there is some as-yet-unknown mental secret that will unlock the vast hidden resources of athletes and allow even an aging jock like me to beat players much younger and stronger. My belief comes from the way my own athletic performance varies so wildly depending on my state of mind. Unfortunately, I've never clearly identified what state of mind leads to increased performance. All efforts to control my mind have been erratic and often frustrating.

When I finally got Dr. Amberry on the phone, I said, "Anyone who can sink 2,750 free throws in a row can tell me how to sink a four-foot putt every single time."

He laughed politely and said he had given up the game of golf years ago. "But," he added, "I can tell you how to focus and concentrate."

Bells went off in my head. I had heard each of these words—focus and concentrate—many times separately. But I had never heard them paired together and spoken by someone who has backed them up with such a remarkable level of performance.

I arranged to meet Dr. Amberry and watch him shoot.

The Rossmoor Athletic Club, in Seal Beach, California, is

where Dr. Amberry practices free throw shooting every morning from 7:00 to 9:00 A.M. I went there to meet him and, on the way to the gym, wound up on the balcony overlooking the basketball court instead of on the gym floor. Out of Dr. Amberry's view, I stood and watched him shoot. I counted to myself as he made 25 free throws in a row. Finally, he turned and saw me and waved me down.

Dr. Amberry greeted me with a warm handshake and a smile that immediately put me at ease. He was completely open and helpful, yet his natural style of speaking gave me answers that were intriguingly brief and loaded with hidden meaning. I felt I was in the presence of a Zen master with a midwestern accent. For example, he suggested I take off my wrist watch when I shot free throws. When I asked him why this helped, he said, "I don't know. But it does."

I asked Dr. Amberry to show me his routine. He described the steps he used, including focusing on the inflation hole as he bounced the ball three times. He handed me the basketball and politely stepped away. I shot my first free throw since being on the eighth grade basketball team. And I missed.

But later that morning I sank 10 in a row. I was pleased with this and credited my relative success to the fact that I had seen Dr. Amberry make 25 in a row. Being in the presence of that kind of ability had raised my performance.

My other memory of that morning is something I hope all readers of this book will experience for themselves. As Dr. Amberry patiently positioned me on the free throw line and made adjustments to my mechanics, I suddenly sank a free throw that gave me an amazing feeling. All the pieces of my body felt like they were working together in just the right combinations. I had the sense that if I could just get into that position each time, the shot would take care of itself. While the setup felt a little awkward, the motion felt absolutely effortless.

Energized by thoughts of focus and concentration I played a round of golf later that week. Golf is probably the ultimate mental game. Sam Snead once said 85 percent of golf is played from the neck up. I had been playing for about a year and a half and was shooting in the low 90s; the previous week I had shot a 93. Two days after talking to Dr. Amberry I shot an 81—my best score ever. In one week I had dropped 12 strokes.

For the following fourteen weeks all my golf scores were in the 80s. I felt I had broken through a barrier. Yet I had not consciously altered my physical game—except for removing my wrist watch, as Dr. Amberry had suggested. What had changed? I asked myself this over and over again, because, of course, I wanted to know how to make this improvement permanent.

Dr. Amberry, or "Dr. Tom" as I learned his friends call him, showed me that your game—whether basketball or golf—can be physically correct in most ways. But if you are not using "focus and concentration" you will never reach your potential. How, then, do you focus and concentrate? This is a question that no one has completely answered. However, Dr. Amberry has come closer than anyone I've ever heard of. How else can you explain 2,750 free throws in a row stretching over a twelve-hour period?

Dr. Amberry would never say that he has solved the mystery of the mental side of sports. But in free throw shooting, where focus and concentration are so desperately needed, he has provided the very best solution. His message is simple: Keep your mind in the here and now; never let it wander away where it might find something in the past or future that will suddenly flash onto the screen of your mind. If this happens, it creates tension in the body that results in a missed shot.

With Dr. Amberry I began to work on a book that would

teach players and coaches a specific free throw shooting routine. In the past, coaches have allowed their players a wide latitude of free throw shooting styles. The key phrase, "what feels most comfortable to you," has guided most choices regarding setup and mechanics. There is one area of overlap in free throw shooting, however. Most coaches agree that the shooters should use the exact same routine each time they go to the free throw line.

The premise of our book is, Why not make your routine the same as Dr. Amberry's? After all, he has a higher free throw shooting average than any other human being who has ever touched a basketball. Am I missing something here? Or does this make good sense?

Coaches and players read early drafts of the book and tested the method with exciting results. But the more we worked on the book, the more we realized we had undertaken a challenging task: to say something new about focus and concentration in general and to teach free throw shooting in particular.

As I continued writing, I began to go with Dr. Tom to the free throw shooting clinics he gave at local high schools and colleges. The first clinic is the one I remember the best. We went to Long Beach Polytechnic High School. This is an inner–city high school with graffiti-splashed walls, razor wire-topped fences, and security guards. The players, mostly African American, looked at Dr. Amberry as if he were a creature from outer space. Their faces seemed to be saying, "What could this old guy teach me that I need to know?"

The first step in winning them over was for Dr. Tom to sink 25 free throws in a row. Perfection got their attention in a hurry. Here's a guy, tall and white-haired, who walks into the gym and sinks 25 in a row from the line. The ball never even touched the rim. They had never seen that before.

Next, Dr. Amberry asked for a volunteer from the team.

No hands. Finally the coach pointed out a young man named Michael who played point guard. He came slouching toward the line full of doubt and resistance. With the rest of the team watching and laughing, Michael missed the first couple of free throws. Then Dr. Amberry got in his face, made eye contact, put his arm on Michael's shoulder and talked softly to him. (Players have said that Dr. Amberry's voice is almost hypnotic.)

Suddenly, a change came over Michael. His entire attitude changed. While focusing all his attention on the shot, his body seemed to relax. The ball went up and into the back of the net. Okay. One free throw is nothing. Same shot the second time. Now he's got some confidence. A third shot. A fourth, fifth, sixth . . . all the way to ten. Now it's someone else's turn.

"Who's going to be the next victim?" Dr. Amberry asks.

All the hands went up.

I saw this happen time after time at clinics. Dr. Tom transforms players. When he leaves the clinics, the kids—once resistant and surly—pump his hand, smiling, filled with gratitude. Sometimes they hug him. Over and over they say the same thing, "Thanks for taking your time to come and help us."

But free throw shooting in practice is only part of the story. It's more about what happens in a game. Dr. Tom knows this and tries to follow up a clinic by going to the team's game. Sometimes, what he sees is discouraging. The players haven't used what he's taught them at all. Under the gun, they've gone back to their old style of free throw shooting.

The excitement of a mental breakthrough somehow loses its appeal. The "secret" we discovered one day seems faded the next time we come out to practice. We begin to buy into conventional "wisdom" that the mind game is beyond our control. And our game suffers.

I practiced my free throw shooting only sporadically while I was writing the first draft of this book. My longest streak was 14 in a row and, once I was warmed up, I could average about 80 percent. But I was stuck. My golf game suffered a similar slump. I went back up into the low 90s and, despite continual tinkering with my physical game, it stayed there.

Then, Dr. Tom and I learned that HarperCollins would publish our book. This was a tremendous boost. I also decided I needed to be more serious about testing the free throw shooting method I was writing about.

I joined the Rossmoor Athletic Club and shot a hundred free throws twice a week and kept track of my results. What I discovered surprised me. While I was consciously aware of what it took to shoot a free throw, and the words on the page were an accurate description of the process, I still hadn't blended them into a reliable routine. My biggest problem was distance control.

Dr. Tom came down to the gym to troubleshoot for me. He pointed out that my knees were fully straightening before my arm launched the shot—my legs weren't contributing anything to my shot. I focused on feeling that all the power was coming from my legs. This took my arm out of it for everything but direction. And my shots began to find the basket with just the right arc.

My other problem was harder to pinpoint. But once I addressed it, the results were more dramatic. After my three bounces, and as I raised the ball into the shooting position, I looked up at the target for too long. By "too long" I only mean maybe a half-second too long. But it was time enough for conscious thought to take control of the situation. I was "aiming."

The solution to this deadly hesitation was to use the seven steps as *one continuous process*. Put another way, I had been thinking of the free throw as beginning when I bent my knees. I began to see that with Dr. Tom's method, the free throw begins when you put your feet square to the line and bounce the ball. It was only then I realized what he had meant by saying he was in a state of auto-hypnosis while shooting a free throw.

The temptation to hesitate with the ball in the shooting position is very strong. A player wants to make sure he or she makes the shot. However, the added effort undoes the benefit of the process. The most accurate view of the basket is that first vivid flash of the target. If, at that moment, we are in position and ready to shoot, our instinct will tell us exactly the right distance and the right direction to send the ball into the basket.

After these two adjustments were made, Dr. Tom stood by and watched as I made 24 free throws in a row, passing my former streak by 10. I then ran laps until I was winded, went to the line, and made two in a row. I did the same thing, went to the other basket, and made five in a row. I felt like I had made a breakthrough. Before long my record for consecutive free throws climbed to 48.

While I was interviewing coaches for this book, many of them, without my prompting, compared free throw shooting to golf and putting in particular. After so many unsolicited comments to this effect, I don't think I'm stretching too far to compare my progress at the free throw line to my golf game.

Soon after making 24 free throws in a row, I headed out to play golf. I suddenly realized that my golf slump was not the cause of bad mechanics but of a faulty memory. I had forgotten that obstacles exist in the mind just as they do in the physical world. My expectations were low—and this brought low results. I told myself to play only one shot at a time. Following this realization, I shot an 84. The following week I shot an 80. What excited me most was I felt it was not a fluke. I had followed the same routine on each shot, controlled my mind, and used the principles of focus and concentration that Dr. Tom had taught me.

What you do with the information and ideas we present in *Free Throw* is up to you. Dr. Amberry and I sincerely hope that you commit to the seven steps and practice them by shooting a hundred free throws a day. We also hope that what you learn about focus and concentration not only improves your free throw shooting and your basketball game but also helps you accomplish anything you really want to do in life.

PHILIP REED
Long Beach, California

Free Throw

1

A Free Throw Is a Gift

If you're going to play at a pro level, you're going to have to take it strong to the hole. If you take it strong to the hole you're going to get fouled. If you get fouled you have to make your free throws.

COLLEGE PLAYER,
LONG BEACH, CALIFORNIA

You get the breakaway pass and you're gone, flying down the court, driving to the hoop. Your eye's on the rim, looking for that game-winning layup.

And then it happens.

You're fouled. Hacked in the act. Sent to the line for two free throws with seconds on the clock and your team trailing by one.

Make one and you tie. Two and you win.

You go to the line. You're winded. Tired. Still mad about the foul. Your teammates' eyes are on you, begging you to make it. The other team is taunting you. *Throw up a brick, man. Air ball. Choke! Choke! Choke!*

The ref hands you the ball. The crowd behind the basket is going nuts.

Two shots stand between victory and defeat. You've made a million free throws in practice. They seem so easy. Just put it up there and watch it fall through the net. But now the rim looks like it's a mile away. The basket is the size of a shot glass. You can't seem to catch your breath. The noise around you is incredible.

You bounce the ball, spin it, look up at the basket, and—

Wait a second! Hold everything! We don't want to start with a negative scenario. You've seen that too many times before. Or, worse yet, maybe it's happened to you.

Instead, I'm going to describe what will happen after you read this book and apply—and practice—my seven steps for free throw shooting success.

WHAT YOUR FUTURE HOLDS

When you're fouled, your first thought is, *No problem. Easy two points.*

You shake off your anger as you walk to the stripe. Then you start your ritual, the ritual you will learn in this book. The seven steps are so ingrained you do them automatically. You square up, bounce the ball three times, and you feel your focus and concentration beginning to sharpen. The noise of the crowd fades. Muscle memory takes over. Your head is clear. You're confident. You shoot and, while the ball's still in the air, you know it's nothin' but net.

Score tied.

Your confidence is strong now. You get the ball again, follow the same ritual. Up and in. You won the game for yourself and your team.

Quit dreaming, you say. Reality is different. Free throws are easy in practice—tough under game pressure. That's just the nature of the beast. And there's nothing you can do about it.

Wrong. The mechanics of free throw shooting can be learned. Combine proper mechanics with focus and concentration and you will be astounded at what you can achieve. I guarantee you will improve far beyond your preconceptions. How much? If you apply what I will teach you, and shoot 100 free throws at every practice, you can be 90 percent from the line.

But, you say, 90 percent is more than most pros shoot. The NCAA average in recent years has only been about 66 percent—and it gets worse every season. Then how can I make such an outrageous promise?

I guess you could say I'm coming from a different perspective. I believe the poor free throw shooting in the NBA and NCAA is the result of two things: poor mechanics and an inability of the players to control their mental game.

Let me put this in broader terms. I am firmly convinced that the only thing limiting you is yourself. That's right. At the age of seventy-three, looking back on a life that included high school and college basketball and a career in medicine, I've come to this conclusion: In everything we do, whether in sports or business or in trying to achieve a life goal, we are more limited by our beliefs than our ability. The obstacles to success exist more in your mind than in the physical world. Nowhere is that simple statement more true than when you stand on the free throw line.

You could almost say that a free throw is a metaphor. It represents all those things in life that are more difficult than they appear. In fact, the harder you try, the more elusive success becomes. Some react by giving up and shying away. Others bear down and eventually succeed. And their success is greater for their struggle.

BE A *COMPLETE* PLAYER

Other sports have situations similar to a free throw in basketball. In football it's a field goal for three points to win the game. In golf it's a four-foot putt on the eighteenth green. In soccer they call them penalty kicks. These clutch plays seem easy in practice yet are difficult under game pressure.

But free throws are unique in one way: the basket is *always* 10 feet above the boards and you *always* stand 15 feet from the hoop. There is nothing between you and the basket. No rushing offense, no breaking curve ball, no spike mark to deflect your putt, no goalie to make a miraculous save.

When you shoot a free throw the only thing between you and the basket is yourself. You stand alone on that line with just your muscles, your heart, and your beliefs. If you miss you get all the blame. If you make it you deserve all the glory.

Sink a free throw and you show yourself, your teammates, and the other team that you are mentally strong. You can take the pressure. Yes, you can dribble and pass and dunk. But unlike so many players these days, you can also make your free throws. It shows everyone your game is *complete*.

Okay, you're convinced. But what can you do? Free throws are a grind. And they never go away. It feels better practicing three-pointers, slam dunks, and jumpers. That may be true, but remember, a champion is someone who excels at things that others find boring and repetitive.

Furthermore, if you want to boost your scoring, the free throw line is the best place to add extra points. And, as I'll tell you later, improving your free throws will improve your three-point accuracy, develop your "shooter's touch," and boost your total game confidence.

Starting today, change your attitude toward free throws. Think of it this way: A free throw is a gift. You were on your way to the basket with a good chance to make a basket or get an assist. The other team illegally took away your chance to score. Now it's payback time. Seize this chance to be in complete control—the basket's wide open, no one in your face. Get the gift that's yours.

FREE THROWS WIN GAMES

Ask any coach how important free throws are and you're apt to get this response: "Free throws win games." UCLA Coach Jim Harrick said he estimates the importance of free throws to be 23 percent of a regular season game and 33 percent of a championship game. He added, "If you can't shoot free throws, you're a hindrance to your team."

Free throws contribute points throughout the game. But those points become more precious as time runs out. The players become desperate in the final seconds of the game. Rather than let the best shooters fire away, they are fouled and forced to shoot from the charity stripe. Furthermore, free throws can start streaks, shift the momentum, and build confidence.

Some of the greatest players are notoriously bad at free throws. In a 1995 playoff game, Shaquille O'Neal, the league's highest-paid player, went 0 for 8 in free throws. Nick Anderson missed four in a row in the final seconds during the same series. This prompted *Sports Illustrated* to write: "Mama always said there are two great imperatives in life: Eat your carrots and make your free throws. Failure to do the latter, as this season's NBA playoffs have made clear, usually assures defeat."

If the other team finds you can't shoot from the line,

you'll be there all night. They won't let you shoot from the floor. If you prove you are strong at the line, they will have to let you shoot. Knowing this will improve your follow-through and release. You know you won't get hacked by some burly point guard as you launch a field goal or get stuffed as you take an inside jumper.

Some of the college players I've coached tell me they try to draw fouls in the beginning of the game. If they can drill a couple of free throws, it builds their confidence and helps them find their rhythm and touch. They take that confidence back into the game and hit more baskets from the floor.

If you need numbers to be convinced, consider this: The national average for free throw shooting in the NCAA is only about 66 percent. A team gets about 700 free throw attempts in a 32-game season. If the players are only average, they will score 462 points. If they improve to my recommended figure of 90 percent accuracy, they will get an additional 168 points. Spread that over the season and that's five extra points per game.

Now think back. How many games did you lose last year by five or less? More free throws each game could have turned those losses into victories. It could have transformed a losing season into a winning season. That's a huge payoff for a little extra practice each day.

A LOST ART

If, as Coach Harrick estimates, free throws are 23 percent of normal season games, than it stands to reason that players and coaches would devote 23 percent of their practice time to perfecting free throw shooting. This obviously isn't the case. Watch any game on TV and the free throw shooting is just plain awful. It's gotten to the point where commentators—and even spectators—whine continually about how these easy points are thrown away.

What's going on here?

Last summer I asked Jerry Tarkanian why the free throw shooting average in the NCAA was so low. His answer was simple and honest: "I think very few coaches really know how to teach free throw shooting."

I'm here to help change that. I believe the mechanics of successful free throw shooting can be learned. Add to this the ability to focus and concentrate under pressure, and you will become a hero at the line.

How do I know all this? What are my credentials?

Last year I shot free throws against Dick Vitale at the Final Four in Seattle. The announcer introduced me as "the greatest free throw shooter ever to touch a basketball." It amazed me to hear it put that way. And yet, here I was, being cheered by thousands of fans. All I could think was, "How in the world did I get here?"

MY FIRST BASKETBALL CAREER

My mind jumped back to Thanksgiving Day, 1939, in Grand Forks, North Dakota, when I was fifteen years old. A blizzard was raging outside. But I was in a warm gym, rebounding for Harold "Bunny" Levitt, at that time the world's greatest free throw shooter. His record was unbelievable—499 free throws in a row!

Bunny Levitt, an underhand free throw shooter, was one of the original Harlem Globe Trotters. He was like a god to me because I wanted to be a great basketball player.

I was always a good shooter. That's because I practiced constantly. I spent all my spare time shooting baskets at a hoop nailed up on the side of the barn, even when there was ice and snow on the ground. When it was just too bad to go outside, I shot at a mark I had made over the kitchen door.

My love of sports probably came from my father, a tough Welshman who was born in Cardiff and moved to Grand Forks where he married and started a family. He loved to play baseball and box. He even fought professionally before I was born. But he didn't think much of basketball. The shorts and T-shirts made him think we were a bunch of sissies. I sometimes wonder what he would think of today's NBA stars.

My father used to call himself a "freight operator" on the railroad. This really meant he unloaded box cars. But during the Depression he lost his job, like so many of the men in our area. He finally found work as a bodyguard for the foreman of a WPA roadworks project. The foreman needed protection because he was Japanese and the local German and Russian immigrants thought this "foreigner" (who had actually gotten a degree at an East Coast Ivy League school) was taking jobs away from them.

I grew seven inches taller than my barrel-chested father. And I was so thin it hurt to look at me. In high school I was 6'7" and weighed only 152 pounds. I was too thin for football although I played it along with baseball and basketball. My performance on the high school basketball team got me a scholarship at Concordia College in Moorhead, Minnesota, 100 miles away from home.

Things might have turned out differently if I had stayed in college and kept playing basketball. But the Japanese bombed Pearl Harbor, and I enlisted in the U.S. Navy. I had tried to enlist several years earlier but was rejected for being too tall. After war broke out the recruiting agent told me to "slouch down a little," and I was accepted. For the next three and a half years, the prime years for an athlete, I was sailing the Atlantic and Pacific Oceans on a destroyer.

After the war I played basketball at the University of

North Dakota from 1945 to 1946. The next season I transferred to Long Beach City College, where I averaged 19.7 points a game, making me All-American that year. I was also highest scorer in the nation for two years. I don't remember much about my free throw shooting performance. But recently, I looked up my college record and found I was 80 percent from the line.

Later I played for the American Basket League's San Diego Tecate Dons and the Oakland Bittners. This was supposedly an amateur league, but the team owners arranged "jobs" for us. I never found out what my job was, even though I was paid well. In fact, there was a joke among players that they would like to join the up-and-coming NBA but they couldn't afford the cut in pay.

After City College I was offered a two-year, no-cut contract with the Minneapolis Lakers for $10,000 a year. It seemed like a fortune then, and I was tempted by the chance to become a recognized professional. It was a tough decision for me, since I loved basketball so much. But by this time I was in my mid–twenties, and I felt my best ball-playing years were already behind me.

I decided to go to the California College of Podiatric Medicine in San Francisco. I became a podiatrist because I thought it would bring me back in touch with athletics. That didn't happen, although I treated many athletes, including Wilt Chamberlain. But I never regretted becoming a foot doctor. I can almost say I enjoyed going to work. I got married, raised four boys, and enjoyed a successful practice in Long Beach, California, where I still live.

BEGINNING MY "SECOND CAREER"

In 1991, when I retired after forty years in practice, I made a startling discovery. I found I had no hobbies. I loved my work so much that podiatry had, in a sense, been my hobby. I soon found that I had too much spare time and too little to do. I mean, how many times can you vacuum the carpet and get a sense of satisfaction from it?

One day, a friend of mine who had also played college basketball asked me to shoot some baskets. I agreed and, at the age of seventy, I picked up a basketball again for the first time in forty years. I soon joined a health club and decided to shoot baskets regularly to get back in shape.

To get to the basketball gym at the Rossmoor Athletic Club, in Seal Beach, California, you have to climb up a long flight of stairs. When I finally got to the gym that first day, I was puffing and wheezing so badly I could barely shoot 50 free throws.

Lou Chavez, who happened to be shooting there that day, later told me: "When I saw you walk in, I thought, 'Man, he's gonna collapse and die right here.' I mean, you were in bad shape. And when you left a few minutes later, I was sure I'd seen the last of you. But no, you showed up the next day. And the next."

My stamina slowly increased, and so did my ability. I've always enjoyed competing, and I wanted to test myself against other basketball players. Obviously, I couldn't run up and down the court and compete against men in their twenties or thirties. But I could stand on the free throw line and compete on an even playing field against younger men. That's what's so good about free throw shooting—it doesn't discriminate against us seniors. Strength and speed don't enter into it. It's a matter of learning to control yourself and your muscles under pressure.

In fact, I soon began to realize that, once you master the basic mechanics, the rest of free throw competition is mental. That's why free throw shooting is so poor in pro basketball now. A player may recognize how psychological free throw shooting is but be at a loss to know how to improve. Although some advances have recently been made, the mental side of sports is voodoo to most athletes—it's a dark and mysterious area few want to enter. But to be a real champion, you have to master the mental side, just as you have the physical side.

After a few months of practice, I began competing in free throw tournaments around the country. Using sheer willpower combined with natural ability and practice, I did pretty well. But it always bugged me when I missed. If I could make 24 in a row, why not 25? I began to wonder if there was a way to guarantee that I could sink a basket every time.

Practice was my first solution. I practiced so much that my left arm gave out. I could barely lift it above my shoulder. I'd always had a good right-handed shot too, so I switched to my right hand and continued practicing.

While competing I had the opportunity to meet and talk with other shooters and coaches about their techniques. Mike Scudder, who played at St. Joseph's College in Rensselaer, Indiana, and gives free throw demonstrations, taught me to keep my feet square to the line and bounce the ball three times to keep the blood moving through my hands and arms. John Scott, who produces instructional videos on basketball, taught me to keep my elbow in. And Buzz Braman, Shaq's former shooting coach, taught me to keep my eye fixed above the rim while the ball is in flight.

I started experimenting with these elements and putting the pieces together in different ways. Eventually I added a few things I made up on my own.

Pretty soon I felt I had the right mechanics. My percentage was steadily improving. But I still missed occasionally. When I missed it bugged me. I knew then that, while I had trained my body, I hadn't trained my mind.

ON THE SPORTS COUCH

When you reach the top of any professional sport, the improvements come slowly and are much more difficult to achieve. This is particularly true with free throw shooting. Lots of basketball players can knock down free throws in practice, but they shoot poorly in the game. Obviously, the problem isn't physical—they proved that by making one free throw after another in practice. The problem is mental.

My search for the perfect free throw method went in a new direction—inward. I began talking to sports psychologists and psychiatrists. Some of the sports psychologists I met were way out there. One guy wanted me to visualize that there was a bug on the back of the rim and I had to squash it with the basketball. But I don't want to put them down. I've always felt if you keep your mind and ears open, you can learn something from almost everyone.

While competing at a senior's event in the Northwest, I met Floyd Strain, a sports psychologist from Payette, Idaho, who has trained numerous Olympic medalists. He really inspired me. He made me believe that there was no limit to my ability. What greater thing can a coach do for a player?

Coach Strain also gave me an image I use every time I shoot a free throw. It is part of my ritual, and I will explain it more fully in the next chapters. But for now, I'll just say that I visualize my arm as being 15 feet long, and I see my hand dropping the ball through the basket. This is the last thing I do before I shoot because it removes all anxiety from my mind. I mean, if your arm was 15 feet long, you wouldn't worry about missing, would you?

DISCOVERING THE SECRET

Up to this point you may be thinking that my free throw method is just a combination of things I collected from players and coaches. To some degree you are right. That's why I wanted to give credit to the people who helped me.

There is one element, though, that I did invent. One day I was thinking of the importance of repetition in free throw shooting. You have to do everything the same way every time. I began to wonder how I could make sure I was holding the ball the same way every time. I couldn't use the markings on the ball because I might get in a competition where they used a different manufacturer's ball.

Finally, I realized what the only universal element is on a basketball—the little round rubber inflation hole. I decided I would put my thumb in the "channel," or groove, so that my middle finger was pointed straight at the inflation hole. Then I would know my hand was positioned correctly. I began to practice this new move. As I bounced the ball, I looked down at the inflation hole. Then, as I caught the ball after the final bounce, I put my hand in position, still looking at the inflation hole.

Soon, I realized I had discovered something much more important than just a consistent way to hold the ball. I found that the small act of looking at the inflation hole held my attention in one place for the length of time it took to shoot a free throw. I called this state of mind "focus and concentration."

Ever since then, the inflation hole has been my symbol for "focus and concentration." Chinese philosophy has the yin and yang symbols. Nike has its elegantly simple logo. And I have the inflation hole.

MY PERCENTAGE CLIMBS

Even with proper mechanics and my technique for focus and concentration, I still had to put it all together in a process that could be repeated. I began shooting 500 free throws a day, in increments of 25—a routine I still do every morning.

As I improved, I kept setting new goals. One day, I heard on the radio that, according to the census, there were nine million men in America my age. I remember thinking, "I'd like to be one of the ten best seventy-year-old free throw shooters in the country." I felt that goal would challenge me, but it was still attainable.

My percentage climbed to 90 percent, then higher. I often made 25 in a row. Then 50. I kept telling myself, if you can make 50, why not 100? If I can make 100, why not 500? Finally, one day, I made all 500 free throws. I walked out of the gym like I had discovered the secret of the universe.

I knew I needed a new goal. I stopped at the local library and looked up the world's free throw record in *The Guinness Book of Records*. What I discovered amazed me: The world record was 2,036, set by Ted St. Martin in 1977. At first I was intimidated. But then I thought, "If he can do it, why can't I?"

On the days when I made all 500, I kept shooting to see how long I could go at 100 percent accuracy. On two separate occasions I shot 2,500 without missing. In both cases, I didn't end on a miss. I had other things to do so I left. I knew I had beaten the world's record—unofficially. But it gave me the confidence I needed for my next goal.

GOING FOR THE RECORD

On November 15, 1993, a few days after I turned seventy-one, I began shooting for the all-time record and my place in *The Guinness Book of Records*. I had hired ten people to be there for the entire day to witness every shot I made. At the end of the event, I would ask them to sign a sworn affidavit saying they had seen every single shot go through the basket.

I soon fell into the familiar rhythm I experienced in practice. *Bounce bounce bounce . . . swish. Bounce bounce bounce . . . swish. Bounce bounce bounce . . . swish.*

My counter announced the baskets as I shot: "256 . . . 257 . . . 258 . . ." Then, suddenly, I remember him saying, "533 . . . 534 . . . 535 . . ." I thought, "Holy smokes! What happened to all those baskets in between?" I had no recollection of them. I was concentrating so deeply I was in a trance.

Of course I had to take short breaks to rest, eat a light snack, and go to the bathroom. But other than that, I shot for over ten hours before I approached the previous record of 2,036. Instead of getting tense, I became increasingly determined to be successful. Then, when I finally heard the counter say, "2,037 . . ." an amazing thing happened. The basket opened up to twice its size! It looked huge! I felt I couldn't miss. I just kept throwing it up there and watching the ball drop in.

After shooting for twelve hours and reaching 2,750 consecutive baskets, I stopped. It wasn't because I missed. They were closing the gym so we all had to leave. But my record was official. You can find my name in the 1996 *Guinness Book of Records*.

THE POWER OF THE PRESS

For about six months after I broke the record, no one seemed to notice. I continued shooting 500 free throws a day and traveling to competitions. Then Debbie Arrington from the *Long Beach Press-Telegram* wrote an article about my free throw shooting record. As soon as it went out on the news wire, my phone began ringing off the hook. A reporter from *Sports Illustrated* interviewed me, and a photographer spent six hours getting one photograph of me to use with the article.

Each time a new article appeared, my phone started ringing. I couldn't imagine getting better publicity than the *Sports Illustrated* article. But I was wrong.

In the summer of 1994, David Letterman challenged me to make 200 free throws on his hour-long nightly show. That was a real test of my ability to concentrate. I was used to shooting in a gym, where I could keep the grit off the ball, the sun out of my eyes, and the wind from deflecting the shot. I told Letterman's producers I was an indoor shooter. But when I got to New York I was informed they wanted me to shoot at a hoop they had set up on 53rd Street, which had been blocked off. I guess Letterman wanted my appearance to be a spectacle. During the show he joked about how he enjoyed tying up crosstown traffic.

When I got to my hotel room, I found myself in a first-class suite: full bar, a VCR, and even my own personal fax machine. The writer from *Sports Illustrated* called to say the issue with the article about me was on the newsstand. Of course I wanted to see it right away, so I decided to take a stroll down to the corner to get a copy. I opened my door and found a man standing there. He followed me down to the newsstand, stood by as I bought the magazine, and then followed me back.

Apparently the producers weren't taking the chance that I might wander away and get lost, so they had assigned someone to watch me until showtime.

After Letterman introduced me to the audience, I walked

down a long corridor and out onto 53rd Street. About 300 people had gathered to watch. There was a 35 m.p.h. cross-wind, flashing police lights, and a screaming audience. I shot while wearing two earphones—the live program in my left ear and the producer talking to me in my right ear.

The producer wanted to show me sinking baskets just before and after they cut to commercials. With no warning, the producer would shout: "Shoot! Shoot!" I didn't even have the six seconds I needed to do my ritual. But by the end of the one-hour show I had sunk 238 free throws.

The Letterman show triggered appearances on all the networks and on "NBA Inside Stuff." Now, when I go into a restaurant people come up to me and say, "You're that guy I saw on TV, shooting baskets. How many was it?"

Life is strange. When I started shooting free throws back in 1992, just to give me something to do, I never dreamed any of this would happen. I was planning a peaceful retirement taking care of my grandchildren. Instead I've had two years of fun and glory, logging over 400,000 miles of travel while winning 228 gold medals.

More importantly, I've had a chance to coach high school and college men's and women's players. I've gone from being a foot doctor to becoming a "shot doctor." Actually, I don't call myself that; the sport is already crowded with so-called "shot doctors." A more appropriate nickname for me was coined by a news broadcaster who called me the "Physician of Free Throws."

GETTING RESULTS

When I give clinics I speak to the team as a whole, then I shoot 25 free throws and make them all. This gets the players' attention. Up to that point they may have been thinking, "What's this old guy know?" But you can't argue with 25 free throws in a row. Most players have never seen someone do that.

I don't shoot the 25 free throws just to show off. I do it to make the players believe in what I'm saying. Athletes will never improve until they *believe* they can improve and believe this deeply. This means that their minds have to accept the belief on every level of consciousness. Only then will they perform at the very highest level of their ability.

The results I have seen in high school and college players have been amazing, even to a veteran positive thinker like me. The coaches always send me their hard cases, good players who have trouble at the line. With fifteen minutes of coaching, I've seen them put together a long string of free throws that has everyone in the gym watching. And that's without any practice at all.

One player on the Long Beach State University '49ers went from 40 percent to 85 percent in a single season. John Welch, now assistant coach under Jerry Tarkanian at Cal State Fresno, shot 68 free throws in a row only a short time after I taught him my technique. Then he made 99 out of 100. The following day, in a league game, he hit six three-pointers in a row—a feat he attributed to his success at the line.

The instant improvement comes from two factors. First, the players have been told they are being coached—one-on-one—by the world's greatest free throw shooter. That alone gives them a lift. The second source of improvement is curing faulty mechanics. For example, if a player has his or her elbow stuck out, I get him to bring it in close. Sometimes I tell them, "Rub your side raw with your shooting elbow." This makes them 50 percent better right away because that takes care of missing shots to the right and the left. And finally, I stress the need for focus and concentration. That's the glue that holds the seven steps together.

The most amazing improvement I've seen so far came one day when I was coaching the Roadrunners at the University of California at Bakersfield. The coach sent me a tall skinny kid who was only 30 percent at the line. It was important that I get results because the local affiliates from CBS, NBC, and ABC were all there taping the session for the nightly news. After showing him my method, making a few adjustments to his mechanics, and boosting his self-image, he began knocking down free throws like you wouldn't believe. He didn't miss until he had made 34 in a row.

The improvement to the Roadrunners as a whole was equally amazing. In their next game, four days later, the team made 30 of 36 free throws. They had entered the game shooting 62 percent from the line; in that game they made 83 percent of their free throws. After the game, CSUB Coach Pat Douglass told the *Bakersfield Californian:* "I guess the vaccine we got [my free throw clinic] didn't take effect for a couple of days." The Roadrunners also won their next two games, both by a narrow margin, maintaining a free throw average above the 80 percent mark.

One of the great pleasures of teaching clinics is hearing how it improves players. High school players often write me, months later, proudly sharing their new free throw averages and the number of free throws they have made in games. They always promise to keep practicing and improving. The letters are personally gratifying, but they are also proof that my method is easily learned and quickly applied.

BE 90 PERCENT FROM THE LINE

I'm living proof that free throw shooting can be taught. Here I am, seventy-three years old, and yet I can beat any NBA star in a free throw contest. I've been challenged by the best, and I always win. That's because I've not only learned the proper mechanics, but I've also learned how to focus and concentrate long enough to make the ball go in the basket—every single time.

When I give a clinic on free throw shooting, I begin by telling the players, "A free throw is a gift." Free throws have brought me many gifts, and a lot of enjoyment. The greatest gift is that I've discovered a new chapter to my life. I ran into Lou Chavez recently, the guy who was in the gym the first day I started shooting. He said, "You've come a long way, man. Your arms and legs have good muscle tone, your color is good. What's your secret?" The secret is, when you find something you love doing, the years drop away. And when I share my love of basketball, I can overcome any age or cultural difference. For me, basketball is a universal language.

Now I have a gift for you. In the following pages, I'm going to tell you everything I've learned about free throw shooting and some other things that I've picked up in the course of a long and satisfying life. If you practice and apply what I tell you, every trip to the free throw line will bring you—and your team—the success you deserve.

2

The Mechanics of
Free Throw Shooting

Chauvinistic Yanks once derided foreign players as "mechanical." Americans should be so mechanical. It's no accident that coaches refer to the elements of shooting as mechanics.

SPORTS ILLUSTRATED

Many basketball players shoot a free throw as if it were just an ordinary shot from the floor. But you'll sink more free throws if you treat it as a set shot with specific mechanics and precise mental demands. Let me go one step further. Free throw shooting is so different from the rest of basketball that it would help you to consider it a "game within a game."

Some of you will recognize that this is a phrase I borrowed from golfers who use it to describe putting. In golf, a good tee shot sends the ball 250 yards. On the same hole the golfer may be required to sink a delicate little four-foot putt. These two strokes will feel very different and may even seem to have no connection. But accurate putting is essential to good scoring. The same is true in basketball. While the free throw bears little resemblance to the rhythm and energy of the rest of the game, you must make your free throws in order to excel as a player and win as a team.

Please keep this "game within a game" concept in mind as you read the rest of this chapter because I am going to be asking you to change your shooting style at the line. These changes will create a new shot in your arsenal, one that is suited for a specific and crucial aspect of basketball.

WHY FREE THROWS ARE TOUGH

The biggest difference between free throws and other basketball shots is that free throws aren't spontaneous. It's not like a shot where you beat your guy, put it up—and watch it drop in for two. In that case you're operating on sheer reflex. You sense an opening, move, and shoot without thinking about it.

With a free throw you have ten seconds—an eternity during game action—to make the shot. No one's in your face. You even know exactly how far you are from the basket. You would think all this would make it easier. But it's just the opposite. When you put too much importance on a simple action it becomes difficult.

If a one-foot-wide plank was lying on your bedroom floor, you wouldn't have any trouble walking along it. But put the plank between two high-rises, forty floors above the city streets, and you would begin to coach yourself on putting one foot in front of the next—something you've done most of your life.

So your first step to increasing your free throw percentage is to recognize it as unique. Remember, it's a gift, your payback for a basket you might have made. Accept the fact that it brings a unique opportunity, along with a special challenge.

A coach I once met said he gave his players this advice: "When you go to the line, say to yourself, 'Stop! Now get set.'" In other words, separate this shot from the flow of the game action. Create a brief, isolated period of concentration to accomplish your task—namely, two points for yourself and your team.

A TON OF BRICKS

The free throw averages of college and pro players are going down every year. Why? As I said earlier, I think the free throw should be a set shot, which was widely used until about fifteen years ago. Now, players don't use the set shot very often in the game.

The set shot was once considered the most accurate way to sink a basket from the outside. If a player found himself unguarded for a moment, he could quickly get into position—both feet on the floor, elbow in, ball below the player's head—and launch the ball straight at the basket.

If no one was covering you, why shoot a jumper? It was extra motion that might throw the shot off track. But as defensive players became more aggressive, the jump shot became dominant. Players began to shoot from above their heads with their elbows out. Otherwise the ball would be stripped or the shot blocked.

Now, most players try to shoot their free throws like a jumper. Their elbow is stuck out, shoulders turned, and they start the shot with the ball above their heads. With my free throw shooting method, I'm bringing the set shot back. I think it is the most stable, accurate way to shoot a basket when you are unguarded. And you're always unguarded at the free throw line.

BUILD A RITUAL

It is critically important to shoot all your free throws in exactly the same way. Your movements should become so repetitive the process actually becomes a ritual.

Ritualization is successfully used in other sports, particularly in situations where it's up to one player to initiate the action. Watch a tennis player who's about to serve. They set their feet, bounce the ball, spin the racket in exactly the same order. Golfers are big on what they call their "pre-shot routine" right down to the way they breathe. Some of their motions have a purpose, such as lining up the shot, while other parts of their routine merely increase their sense of feel and rhythm before starting the swing.

A free throw shooting ritual is valuable for several reasons. It gives you something to focus on other than the pressure you are under. Instead of thinking about the score, or the number of fouls you have, or the time on the clock, focus on the steps in your ritual. If you do the steps correctly, the result will take care of itself.

As you practice this free throw shooting ritual, you may find you have to remind yourself to do all seven steps. In other words, you have to lead yourself through the ritual. But in the game, when you're under pressure, the ritual will lead you to do the right thing. While your mind is trying to go in a million directions, the ritual will bring you back to the task at hand; it will bring you back to the present—and help you sink your free throws.

The ritual triggers rehearsed movements from certain muscle groups. It's like a wake-up call to your body. When you step to the line, you will do what you have done hundreds of times in practice. Your muscles will seem to say, "I remember this." Then, if you keep your mind clear, your body will take over and do what it's been trained to do.

Ritualization also eliminates decisions. Making a decision in the game, with the clock running, is one thing. You're operating on sheer instinct and reflex. But decisions at the free throw line create doubt. And, as any player will tell you, doubt and uncertainty lead to mistakes and missed shots. When you go to the line, every level of your mind and every muscle in your body have to know *ahead of time* what to do to make that basket. You should *feel* the shot going into the basket before you even shoot the ball.

STYLE OR SUBSTANCE?

Basketball is filled with style. Certain moves are passed down from the pros to the college and high school players. If Michael Jordan shoots his jumpers with his tongue out, pretty soon kids in playgrounds across the country are doing the same thing.

Players imitate each other's moves at the free throw line, too. The pros spin the ball, put it behind their back or do some quick dribbling before they shoot. The younger players see this and copy their sports heroes.

I think players use these moves to try to bring back a feeling of the game rhythm. If they stay loose in a game, they can shoot better. So they do the same thing at the line. But, as I mentioned earlier, free throw shooting is a game within a game. It is separate from the rest of basketball. Trying to recreate a game feel here won't always work.

Instead, your movements at the line should be slower and more deliberate. That's why I think these fancy moves hurt a player's concentration. The focus should be on preparing to make the shot, on getting into a special state of mind, and directing all your concentration to the target.

When I'm coaching a player who spins the ball before

shooting, I always ask, "Do you want style or substance?" Use the routine that puts the ball in the basket, not the one that looks good. After the game is over, which will the crowd remember? What will it say in the sports page the next morning? "He missed his free throws but, hey, he had some beautiful moves before he took the shot." I don't think so.

Okay, so you're sold on the value of ritual. But you're wondering what your ritual should be. Well, you're in luck. I spent two years developing the perfect free throw ritual. And now I'm going to tell you exactly what you have to do to put the ball in the basket. But first I want your commitment to trying something that might, at first, seem unnatural.

LEAVING THE COMFORT ZONE

As I talk about the mechanics of free throw shooting, I will probably be recommending some changes to your present style of shooting. Some of these movements may feel unnatural at first. Because they feel different you may be uncomfortable—and this might even make you think the technique is wrong. Let me make something very clear: When you shoot your free throws in the game, I want you to be as comfortable as possible. How do you become comfortable? By practicing the right mechanics *until* the movements become comfortable.

You have to trust me on this one, but after you blend together and practice my seven steps, you will feel more comfortable at the free throw line—because you will know you're about to make two points. Remember what it was like learning to drive a car. You had to consciously remind yourself to step on the clutch when shifting gears. You had to think about all your actions. Do you do that after even six months of driving? No. Those motions have been assigned to other areas of your brain while you think of the big picture—where you want to go.

How long will it take for my method of free throw shooting to feel comfortable? It depends on how much you practice and how deeply you commit to adopting this method. UCLA Coach Jim Harrick says that it takes twenty-eight days to fully integrate a change to your playing style. I've also heard that it's five times harder to break a bad habit than it is to develop a good one. That's why it's important to develop good fundamentals when you're starting to play basketball, rather than making changes when you are older.

Right now you are probably doing some things that are not conducive to sinking free throws (that's why you are reading this book). But you are "comfortable" with your style. It has given you, let's say, a free throw shooting average of 70 percent in practice and 60 percent in games.

The question facing you now is, Do you want to remain comfortable with the wrong mechanics and a low free throw percentage? Or are you willing to be uncomfortable—for a short time—with the *right* mechanics, to eventually improve? Let me put it this way, if you achieved a 90 percent free throw average in practice, would you feel more comfortable going to the line in a tight game than you do now with a 70 percent average? Learn to do it the right way, see the results you get, and your comfort factor will go way up.

SEVEN STEPS TO A PERFECT FREE THROW

I do all of the following seven steps each time I shoot a free throw. The steps are designed to coordinate the physical and mental requirements of free throw shooting. I think of this ritual as my six-second trance. I focus and concentrate just long enough to make the free throws. Then I relax.

Step 1. Feet square to the line.

When I first began practicing free throws, I taped dimes to the floor where I wanted my feet to be. Then I could slide my feet until I felt the tips of my shoes hit the dimes—and I knew my feet were in exactly the right position. There is an easier way to find the right position on the free throw line.

When the lines are painted on a basketball court, the painter drives a nail into the center of the free throw line. A string is tied to this nail and used to draw the circular shape for the top of the key. This little dot is called the "painter's hole" and it is dead center on the free throw line. You can use it to make your shots dead center in the back of the net.

When you're getting ready to shoot a free throw, use the painter's hole to make sure you are centered on the foul line. Straddle the hole, feet about shoulder-width apart, squared to the line. Using the painter's hole will guarantee you are in exactly the same place on the line every time.

I see a lot of players who are "pointers." They have one foot forward pointing at the basket. This may feel more natural—in fact, it's been recommended by some free throw experts. But there are two problems with pointing.

First, with one foot back, your shoulders turn and you can miss the shot to the left or right. Secondly, if you pull one foot back from the line (your left foot for right-handers) you can never set up in exactly the same way each time. There is no line on the floor to position your back foot. Your left foot will always be in a different position. You might say your left foot could only vary in its position by an inch or two. My answer to that is, "Have you ever missed a shot by an inch or two?"

In case you haven't picked this up so far, I'll come right out and say it. In order to get the highest possible free throw average, you have to try to turn you body into a machine. What I'm telling you now will put that machine into the best possible position to score.

Recently I was at a college game, and a coach came up to me and said, "Have you noticed how many pros are squaring up when they take their free throws?" Not only that, but many of the best shooters square up as they take their jumpers. They may say they don't, but if you study pictures, you'll see that as they release the ball, their shoulders and feet are square to the ball's line of flight. Squaring up puts your body in just the right position to go straight at the basket with your shooting arm.

I should also mention that a good free throw shooter has his or her weight forward on the balls of the feet. The body should be leaning toward the basket in a balanced, active stance, not standing straight up. You will actually be closer to your target in this position—and that doesn't hurt either.

Step 2. Bounce the ball three times with the inflation hole up.

When I first started teaching my free throw method, I was invited to work with some of the players on the Long Beach State University '49ers. One player was really struggling at the line, with a free throw shooting average of only 40 percent. After I coached him, he improved dramatically for a while, then began to lose ground again. A friend of mine, who shot my instructional video, also tapes all the '49er's games. One day he reviewed my seven steps with this player and found that, while he was using most of the steps, he had not been looking at the inflation hole to trigger a state of focus and concentration.

Several weeks passed, and the player came up to my friend and said, "You know, I've been using that thing about the inflation hole. Now I'm really kicking butt." This player had been using my technique and getting adequate results, without using the secret that holds it all together. Two days later I read in the sports page that this player hit two free throws in the final minutes of play. According to the sports writer, those free throws sparked a rally that won a tight game.

Let's look at how to use the inflation hole to help you focus and concentrate on making all your free throws. When the ref hands you the ball, turn it so the inflation hole is up. With your eye on this little black rubber dot, bounce the ball slowly three times. Don't dribble the ball. Bounce it slowly and deliberately. This will bring you back to the here and now. It will remind you that this is a different shot, a "game within a game." It will create a quiet, isolated period of concentration where the tempo is different.

Bouncing the ball will keep the blood flowing through your shooting arm and hand. This keeps your muscles relaxed and your movements fluid. You never want to shoot from an absolutely frozen stance. If you do, the first motion is apt to be jerky and exaggerated.

Most players already bounce the ball. So that's not a difficult transition for you to make. But why look at the inflation hole?

In a practical sense, locating the inflation hole guarantees that, when you hold the ball before shooting, you will hold it the same way every time. But looking at the inflation hole is also a mental step. As I said before, the inflation hole is meaningless, completely neutral. Everything else you might look at in the gym would put more pressure on you—the scoreboard, the clock, your coach. So looking at this little round rubber dot will help you clear your mind of all the pressure-producing thoughts that build up during a tight game.

Pretend the inflation hole is the black hole of the universe, gathering up all your scattered thoughts and focusing your concentration into one small point. This, combined with bouncing the ball three times, will clear your mind and allow your ritual to begin. As your ritual begins, your mind and body will work together, not fight each other.

Step 3. Put your thumb in the channel, your third finger pointing at the inflation hole.

No matter how much I've tried to mechanize the shooting process, it ultimately comes down to a sense of *feel*. Your connection to the basketball is your hand, or actually, your fingertips. The ball has to feel good in your hand. When you hold the ball before your free throw, your body should be saying, *Yeah, this feels good—I'm gonna drill this one.*

You've got to hold the ball in some way. Why not hold it the same way every time? The way it feels best, almost molded to your hand. Don't think of the ball as a separate object that resists you. Think of it as an extension of your body—your will—that will obey you even after it's left your finger tips and is arcing toward the basket.

You'll find that when you catch the ball after the third bounce, you can simultaneously put your hand in the correct position. Practicing this move will make the steps blend together smoothly. Put your thumb in the "channel," or groove, in such a way that your third finger is pointed at the inflation hole. Now don't move your hand again. Don't slide your hand around or spin the ball. Your hand is in the best position for shooting right where it is.

Putting your thumb in the channel will also put some rotation, or backspin, on the ball as you release it. You don't have to try to do anything extra. With the correct release from your fingertips and thumb, the rotation will automatically be added to the shot. This rotation can make the difference between shooting a basket and throwing up a brick.

Putting your hand in the correct position will give you the "shooter's touch." What is the shooter's touch? Technically, it's the way you release the ball when you shoot. If you've got the right rotation, the ball lands softly when it hits the rim and drops in for a basket. If you haven't got the touch, the ball accelerates when it hits the rim. It rattles around and jumps out.

After years of shooting baskets, I have to say that the shooter's touch is something above and beyond just rotation on the ball. It's that last little extra bit of *feel* that any great athlete has. It's the feel you get when you love the sport you play. The feel you only develop when you eat, sleep, and drink your sport.

Step 4. Elbow in.

The first three steps have gotten you into the best possible position to sink a free throw. Your mind is clear of extraneous thoughts and you are holding the ball with your thumb in the groove. The next four steps are the actual shooting steps.

I have separated these four motions into separate steps to help you learn, remember, and practice them. In reality, they are interrelated, overlapping, and blending together so smoothly they will seem like one fluid motion, always leading to the basket. This process begins when you bring your elbow into the "shot pocket."

What is the shot pocket? I'll show you how to find it by adopting the motto of many successful people: "Work backward." High achievers see where they want to go, then figure out what steps it will take to get them there. Do that now for free throw shooting.

Set the ball down for a moment. Now take up your stance

straddling the painter's hole on the free throw line. Extend your arm toward the middle of the back rim of the basket. Imagine your arm is 15 feet long. Picture yourself dropping the ball softly through the hoop. Pull your arm back until your hand is in the middle of your chest. Your shooting hand is now on an imaginary line that runs through your body and leads to the center of the basket.

Now pick up the ball, hold it with your thumb in the groove, and put your hand in the same position. If you are like a lot of players, you may still have your elbow out in the breeze somewhere. You need to bring it into position, so your elbow is in the "shot pocket."

There are only four ways to miss a basket: short, long, right, or left. With the correct knee bend (covered in the next step), your distance will be precise and you won't be long or short. Now, if you bring your elbow in and straighten your arm so your fingers go right at the basket, you eliminate missing to the right and left. You've just cut your misses down by 50 percent.

Of all the steps I recommend, bringing the elbow in feels the most unnatural to many players. *But it is also the most important of all the free throw shooting mechanics.*

I often see players shooting from the outside with their elbow stuck out. They do that to ward off defenders who are trying to strip the ball away. But remember what I said earlier: the free throw is different. No one's in your face. You're in complete control. So you want to shoot it the way that will give you the highest consistency. That means bringing the elbow in.

Think about this for a second. When a right hander extends his or her arm with the elbow out while shooting, the ball is pushed across the target, ending with the hand positioned to one side of the basket. To hit the target, you have to release the ball at just that fraction of a second when the hand is in the exact right position. To do this you need extremely good *feel* and *touch*. Those are the first things to desert you when you're under pressure at the free throw line.

When you start the shot with the elbow in, the hand and the ball are traveling right down the line that leads to the basket. While it may feel machinelike at first, that's okay. I want you to turn yourself into a scoring machine. So bring that elbow in and relax—tell yourself that there's no way you can miss right or left.

Step 5. Bend your knees.

Some experts have suggested that free throw shooting should be an upper body movement. I completely disagree. Bending your legs—the same amount each time—will give your shot just the right distance. Then your arm can guide the ball into the basket. If you don't believe me, try shooting while you're sitting in a chair. Sure you can reach the basket. But when you're straining for distance, your accuracy suffers.

When shooting, we tend to forget the legs and overemphasize the arm, hand, and fingertips. That's because the ball is in our hands. We feel it with our fingers. But the shot is actually a series of linked actions that move from the ground up. Not only do you get the right distance with the proper knee bend, you also set up a smooth flow for the actions that follow. The knee bend sends a fluid wave through the whole body that launches the ball toward the center of the basket.

In Wilt Chamberlain's autobiography he says he was a great free throw shooter in high school. But then he injured his knee so that when he bent it while shooting from the line, it hurt him. He changed his free throw shooting method, and his percentage went way down. Throughout his career he was plagued by his reputation as a lousy free throw shooter. He was so distressed by this he actually went to a psychiatrist to find out why he was missing.

There is another good reason to originate the shot from the legs. The big leg muscles are more reliable when you get jitters on the line when shooting a clutch free throw. The movements of the smaller arm, wrist, and hand muscles are apt to be jerky and exaggerated.

How deeply should you bend the legs? You have to experiment. But it will probably be a little more than you think. Bend the legs enough so your arm feels as if it isn't doing any work at all. You'll see that the knee bend naturally adds a nice high arc to the ball, too.

With a good knee bend you will never miss short of the rim. If I were forced to choose, a shot that is too long is better than one that is too short. A long shot still has a chance of going in, even when it banks off the backboard. But an air ball is not only a lost point, it's a complete embarrassment.

Once you find your legs giving the right distance to the shot, groove this feeling and let it blend with the rest of your free throw shot. Remember, the arc of the ball is a combination of the knee bend and the angle at which your arm extends. Let these factors work together smoothly.

One other thing. When you get under pressure, the muscles in the body tighten. This is most noticeable in the legs. You tend to stand stiff-legged when you're under the gun. Just before you begin your ritual, do a couple of knee bends to keep loose. Then, when you get into your routine, your knees will bend just the way they did in practice.

Step 6. Eyes on the target.

Someone once told me that it's not important where you *are* that counts, it's what your sights are set on that will bring you success or failure. You could live in a shack and dig ditches for a living. But if you consistently think of living in a mansion on a hill, working at a dream job, you'll eventually find a way to get there.

In this step, you are going to set your sights on where you want the ball to go and keep them there until you hear the crowd cheer. In other words, before you even shoot the ball, tell your body you are not going to watch the ball in flight. This keeps your body still and sends your mind a powerful message: The ball is going to find the target.

The eyes are powerful motivators of physical motion. If, as you shoot the ball, you are filled with doubt, you will quickly glance at the ball to see where it's going. You might cut off your follow-through—or "pull the string," as it's sometimes described. Your release won't be smooth. The ball will hit the rim like a brick.

Okay, so what should you look at when you shoot?

There have been many theories about where to look when shooting. Your first instinct is to focus on the front of the rim since that's what you see when you look at the basket. But this causes shots to miss short. If you look at the front of the rim, you hit the front of the rim. This doesn't indicate a problem with your shot. The problem is what you are aiming at.

Other shooters say they aim for the back of the rim. But you don't want to hit that either. If you actually hit the rim, you can't be sure that the ball will drop into the basket.

Your target is actually an empty space, a cylinder of air though which you want the ball to drop. Look at the space above the back rim and keep your eyes there until you see the ball drop through it on the way into the basket.

Those of you who are paying close attention may be puzzled by the order of these steps. I have told you to bend your knees, then look up at the target. You might feel that I'm not allowing enough time to look at the target before you shoot.

This is the whole idea. You don't want to look at the target too long before shooting. In fact, you want to shoot while that first image of the basket is flashing onto the screen of your brain. This keeps you from thinking. At this moment "thinking" is the worst thing your could do. Why? What's to think about?

As I've said before, you already know where the basket is. The danger is not having too little time to look at the basket. The danger is looking at the basket so long you interrupt the flow of these interconnected motions.

While writing this book I looked at high-speed videos of my free throw shooting. I found that bringing my elbow in, bending my knees, and looking up at the target all overlapped. It is important to remember the steps. But don't rigidly enforce this order. And don't try to separate them. Let them blend together with your natural rhythm.

Step 7. Shoot and follow through.

Your feet and shoulders are square to the basket, your elbow is tucked in, your knees are giving just the right push to the shot, and your eyes are locked on the target. Your preparation up to this point is so good the shot will almost take care of itself. Notice I said, *almost*.

You still need to extend your shooting arm smoothly from the shot pocket straight at the target. You need to have a good release and make sure your follow-through is complete. However, you have already placed your body in position so that those motions will follow naturally and smoothly.

Why is the follow-through important? You might argue that the only thing that matters is what you do while the ball is touching your fingertips. Once it's gone, who cares what your follow-through looks like? When I was playing college ball, the coach didn't want you to follow through. They thought that was hot doggin'.

But now we know the follow-through is important because it has a strong influence on what comes just before it—the release. If you begin and continue a shot, even when the ball is on its way, you'll guarantee the best arc, backspin and touch. Some coaches even recommend holding your follow-through for one full second after the ball is on its way. This isn't showing off. It will make your movements smooth and complete.

Good free throw shooting comes from smoothly blending interrelated fundamentals. In my seven steps I've focused on the key movements that make up a successful free throw. Now I'd like to comment on several related questions that you might be wondering about.

THE OFF-HAND

The off-hand, or "helper hand," is important because it holds the ball in the right position until the shooting arm provides the push. I like to keep things simple. I don't want to have to think of anything extra. So let's get the off-hand in the right position and then focus on other things.

The easiest way to describe the off-hand is to compare it to a tee in golf. It holds the ball in the right position until the moment that the club strikes it. The tee wouldn't be doing its job if it held the ball in different places or moved it around. In basketball it's the same way. You want stability and consistency from the off-hand.

When your shooting arm is in the shot pocket, much of

the weight of the ball is resting on the off-hand. If you don't like the golf tee analogy, pretend you are holding a tray of food. If you are positioned correctly, your forearms and elbows are close together. As you shoot, your off-hand remains in the same position as your shooting arm straightens.

The off-hand should not change position very much. If it begins to sneak up, following the shooting arm as it extends, you are adding unnecessary motion. The next thing you know, the offhand will be wanting to get into the action. Then you're shooting a jumper and not a set shot.

To be consistent at the line, you have to do everything the same way every time. Keep this helper hand under the ball and close to your body. Check its position in practice to make sure it's not drifting around. Then, in the games, put it out of your mind and focus on your distance and accuracy.

COCKING THE WRIST

Shooting coaches stress the importance of cocking the wrist as you prepare to shoot. The snap that the wrist provides as it straightens is the last motion in shooting a basketball. This motion is valuable because it adds rotation to the ball. As I mentioned earlier, this rotation makes the ball land softly if it hits the rim.

My feeling about the wrist cock is: Why complicate matters? Why add an extra element to the free throw process? If you get the shooting arm into the right position, with the ball close to your body in the shot pocket, the wrist automatically cocks. If you relax and follow through, the wrist will uncock and provide the needed rotation.

Get your basketball and put yourself in the right position to shoot a free throw, with your arm in the shot pocket and your elbow tucked in. Now look at your wrist. Is the skin on the back of your hand wrinkled? Then your hand is cocked. Now relax and forget about wrist cocking.

THE ARC OF A FREE THROW

Shooting the ball with the correct arc is important. But it's hard to prescribe one arc for every player. One player might be six feet tall while the next is 7'3". That's a difference of 15 inches. The arc for these two players should be different, too.

When trying to change your arc, or when looking for the proper arc, you should examine the movements that cause the arc rather than directly trying to control the angle at which the ball leaves your hand. The arc comes from three factors: the power from the legs, the angle of the shooting arm, and the mental concept you hold of the flight of the shot.

Many shooters, even good ones, throw up a flat shot one time, a high one the next. I think this is because, as the shooting motion progresses through the body, you sense whether the push from the legs is strong enough. If it is, the arc is good and the shot probably swishes through the net. But if the legs don't do their job, you try to compensate by shooting harder with your arm. You tend to push the ball at the basket rather than shooting it with a smooth follow-through. Sometimes you get lucky and drill it. Other times the ball hits the front of the rim.

My experience has shown me that, as you practice, your arc should be a little higher than you think it needs to be. This would probably be a medium arc of between 35 and 45 degrees. A medium arc allows for better control and closely matches the natural shooting style of most players. With this arc a perfect shot will hit the back of the net. If it hits the rim, it still has a good chance of dropping in.

Naturally, you will need to adjust your arc if you are having trouble hitting the target. You might have the right force behind the shot, but if the arc is too high or too flat, the ball will miss the basket. So instead of adjusting the power behind the shot, change your arc. If the shot is long, raise the arc; if the shot is short, lower the arc.

Let me give you a simple way to adjust the arc of your free throws. It may seem strange, but this can be accomplished by changing the way you *think* about the shot. To keep my arc just right, I look at the space above the basket and imagine the ball going into the hoop. This creates the right mental picture of the ball clearing the front rim and dropping into the net. It helps me produce shots that have a nice natural loft without tying myself in knots analyzing trajectories and angles.

The words you use to think about sports are important. Rick Barry, who was a great shooter, says that too many players think about shooting "at" the basket. Then, the ball isn't shot, it's pushed. The ball is often short and hits the front of the rim. Instead, he thinks of shooting "up to" the basket. I think this is good advice. If I didn't already have my key thought, I might change.

However you achieve your arc, just remember: The arc you put on the ball should be a natural product of your shooting style. Shoot to make the basket, not to put a specific arc on the ball.

ONE FLUID MOTION

After reading this you might feel like you now have a lot of things to remember. I didn't develop these steps to give you "paralysis of analysis." I did it for one reason: to score more points from the line. And if your free throw shooting improves, the rest of your game will improve, too. Confidence breeds success. And success breeds more confidence.

It should take you about fifteen minutes to learn to blend all these steps together into one fluid motion that takes six seconds to execute. At the clinics I teach, the coaches always send me their worst free throw shooters to work with. I've seen amazing improvement in only ten or fifteen minutes. It's as if they have been waiting for clear instructions to follow. Once they learn the routine, the ball finds the basket over and over again.

When all the pieces of my process come together, you'll feel something special. You'll get to the point where you will know the ball is in the basket as it leaves your fingertips. That's the *zone*. And you can be there every time. You're only three bounces away. Start your ritual and let it happen.

The more you are able to blend these movements, the more fluid your motions, the more free throws you'll hit. By all means find your own rhythm and pace. But before you begin adapting and changing what I've described, remember: I spent two years adding and modifying these steps. I spent over two months on a single motion. When I put it all together, I made 2,750 free throws and walked away without a miss. If you think you've found something that I've overlooked, and you beat my record, I'll be happy to listen to you. Until then, I'm convinced this is the best way to shoot a free throw.

Here's a page for you to cut out and put in your pocket before you head for the courts next time. Learn it. Practice it. Stick with it. And make every free throw.

SEVEN STEPS TO A PERFECT FREE THROW

1. Feet square to the line.
2. Bounce ball three times with the inflation hole up.
3. Thumb in channel, third finger pointing at the inflation hole.
4. Elbow in.
5. Bend your knees.
6. Eyes on the target.
7. Shoot and follow through.

3

The Mental Side: Focus and Concentrate

The past and the future are the enemies of the athlete.

Dr. Mark Boyea,
Performance Development Associates

Here is something that may help you become a better free throw shooter right away.

Picture yourself putting a ruler across the rim of the basket. It would show that the basket is 18 inches across. Now measure the ball. It's a little more than nine inches across. You could almost stuff two basketballs through the hoop at the same time.

This means that in a dead perfect shot, there are four and a half inches all around the ball. In fact, you could have only one inch on one side and eight on the other and still have a swish. The margin of error in shooting a free throw is much greater than you may have imagined. This may come as a surprise because, when we look at the hoop high above us, it is partially obscured by the net. In fact, I've related these dimensions to longtime basketball players and had them say, "Man, I thought the ball just squeaked through there."

My description of the basket may have created a new impression in your mind. At this moment, it would probably be easier for you to sink a free throw. Why? Has the basket become any larger? Have you become a better shooter? No. Your perception of the difficulty has been reduced.

This is an example of the importance of the mental side of basketball, and it will begin to show you the importance of controlling your thoughts while you're at the free throw line. Always minimize the difficulty and maximize your own abilities.

There is a paradox when you consider controlling your thoughts. The only thing that controls the mind is the mind itself. In Leslie Nielsen's *Stupid Little Golf Book* he says that it's very important *not* to think while you're playing golf. The problem is that you have to remember not to think. And that, of course, makes you think.

Once you get caught in this cycle of reasoning, *not* thinking seems impossible. But there is a way to get control of your thoughts if you understand a little about how the mind works.

ONE THOUGHT AT A TIME

Sometimes our minds seem hopelessly cluttered. While we are capable of many thoughts in rapid succession, we can only have one thought in our conscious mind at a time. Make that thought negative and you are paving the way to failure. But make that one conscious thought positive and you have greatly increased your chances of succeeding.

If you accept this simple concept and learn to apply it, it will not only make you a great free throw shooter, it will help you achieve anything you really want to do in life.

In the final seconds of a game, when you go to the line with two free throws to win or tie, that single conscious thought must be positive. As strange as it might seem, you *can* use your mind to control your mind. You do this by using the secret of focus and concentration.

I know, I know—you've heard this before. Coaches are always yelling *Concentrate! Concentrate!* But they don't tell you *how* to concentrate. Or even what concentration is.

THE POWER OF FOCUS AND CONCENTRATION

Pick up the sports page any morning and read the quotes of sports stars. Many of these winners attribute their success to concentration. Others say they won because they were focused. These words—*focus* and *concentrate*—jump off the page. I've gone one step further by putting the words together as a winning pair: focus and concentration.

These are familiar words to most people, but they are used in many different ways. Let me tell you how I think they apply to the world of sports in general, and free throw shooting in particular.

One meaning of *focus* is to see things clearly. When you focus your vision, the lens in your eye draws rays of light together to make a sharp picture. A magnifying glass can focus light to a tiny point where it becomes so hot it will start a fire. For an athlete to catch fire, so to speak, all his or her attention needs to be focused on that moment. I'm not suggesting that the athlete's mind needs to be engaged in analyzing movements or techniques. That's for practice. All I'm saying is that the mind should be used to hold the athlete's attention comfortably in the present—in the here and now. Why is this important?

Let's say you're standing on the free throw line at the end of a close game waiting for the ref to hand you the ball. You look up at the scoreboard and see there are only ten seconds to play and you're down by two. If your mind is unfocused, your thoughts might leave the present and drift back to a similar game, perhaps in high school, in which you went to the line and missed two to cost your team the championship. Your mind begins to recall more specifics about that incident: the agony that followed that loss, the look on your coach's face after the game, the groan of the crowd, the cheers of the opposing team.

At the end of this scenario, you are apt to say to yourself, "I never want to go through that again! I *can't* miss this shot."

Now, back to the present. The ref hands you the ball and you're about to shoot with those thoughts still lingering in your mind. How do you think your body is reacting? Are your muscles tight? Is your heart pounding? You bet it is. You put so much pressure on yourself, you feel that the world will come to an end if you miss the shot.

When you speculate about the future you begin to play a dangerous game. There are many things about the future that are uncertain and out of your control. On the other hand, the outcome of past events is known, but they are unalterable. There is a saying that is bouncing around the country now that sums this up: "Yesterday is history, tomorrow is a mystery. Today is a gift—that's why they call it the present."

Remaining focused means keeping your mind in the here and now and dealing with those things you are in control of. And, as I said before, the free throw line is one of the few situations in basketball where you are always in complete control.

A CONCENTRATED SOLUTION

I consider concentration to be the partner of focusing. Concentration has also come to mean different things to different people. First, let me describe what concentration is, before I discuss what it *is not*.

When a liquid solution of anything becomes stronger, it becomes more concentrated. The only thing that has changed is the strength of the liquid. No new ingredients have been added. For a basketball player concentration means using the mind to become a stronger player. With concentration you are the same person, with the same qualities, but you are a stronger, more effective player.

While this may help you understand concentration, it doesn't necessarily help you apply it any better. When I tell players that concentration is needed at the free throw line, this is what I get: The player raises the ball into the shooting position and then freezes. He or she stares at the basket for several seconds and then awkwardly throws up a shot, which often misses.

Concentration doesn't mean "trying hard." It doesn't mean gritting your teeth or staring at the target until your eyes are ready to pop out. Concentration may, in fact, be just the opposite of what most people think it is. I'm taking some liberty here, but let me say that concentration in basketball is using your mind to maximize your abilities to achieve the highest degree of success.

Don't let concentration add to your problems by filling your body with tension. Use concentration instead to become strong and successful.

In the rest of this chapter, I'm going to tell you how to use these magic words—*focus* and *concentration*—to train your mind, in the same way the previous chapter told how to train your body. Let me begin by telling a story that will convince you that the mental side of free throw shooting is as important as using the correct shooting mechanics.

GETTING MENTALLY READY

Setting the world's free throw record involved a lot more than nailing a hoop on the side of a barn and counting baskets. I had to pay ten people to watch every single shot go through the hoop and sign sworn affidavits as witnesses to the event. Only then did *Guinness* accept what I had achieved as an official world's record.

Since I was going to so much time and expense, I wanted to be certain I would break the world's record. I didn't want to get up to 75 baskets and throw up a brick. Or worse, get close to the previous record of 2,036 and fall apart. What if my 2,035th shot rimmed out?

I had to create the most favorable mental conditions possible. I had to sustain my concentration for twelve hours. To accomplish that, I tried an experiment on myself that proved to be very successful.

There are a lot of things about the state of the world that upset me. Often, I read something in the morning paper that sticks with me all day, suddenly invading my mind and disturbing my train of thought. I didn't want this to happen when I was approaching the goal I'd set.

So, for three weeks before my record attempt, I began a very specific mental diet. I eliminated all unpleasant and controversial thoughts from my mind. I stopped reading the newspaper. I stopped listening to talk shows on TV and on the radio.

Instead, I listened to beautiful music. I put on tapes of my favorite comedians. I read inspirational books. I let my mind dwell on humorous, harmonious, and pleasant thoughts exclusively for three weeks.

My reasoning was this: The mind is complicated and mysterious. Much of it is beyond our direct control. It takes a long time to condition the mind or change thought patterns. I felt that a minimum of three weeks would be required to push all the upsetting and confrontational thoughts to a low enough level so that for twelve hours my mind and body could be in complete harmony.

Think about what this means for a moment. I treated my mind the way most athletes condition their bodies. I was very careful about what I fed my consciousness. For at least short periods of time, I thought, I could control what I put into my mind.

What I did was try to create the best possible circumstances for success. If you can deeply believe in your own ability, you will win. But attaining that level of belief is almost as difficult as the sport itself.

In boxing, the will to win is often described as "having heart." Spectators see this in the ring when a fighter keeps punching and won't give up. But did you know that you can see this quality long before the fight starts?

A friend of mine, Michael De Luca, M.D., a sports psychiatrist, and physician for the California State Athletic Commission, examines the fighters in their dressing rooms before the match. He says he can tell by looking into the eyes of the two boxers which of them will have his hand raised in victory at the end of the fight. Their heart, their belief in themselves as winners, is as clear as their physique, their skill, and their speed.

POSITIVE TEACHING

The need to maintain a positive attitude was also recognized by the great golf instructor Harvey Penick. He said he always avoided using the word *don't* when he was giving lessons. Instead he flipped the sentence around to state things positively. He wouldn't say, "Don't bend the left arm."

He would suggest, "If you keep the left arm straight your distance and accuracy will improve."

Penick avoided using certain words altogether, such as the athlete's most dreaded term for failure under pressure: *choke*. Instead of saying, "Choke down on the club when chipping," he would say, "Grip down on the club." He didn't want the word *choke* to be in a student's consciousness in any context.

Like Penick, I think that our thoughts affect our actions. I believe that the body is the servant of the mind. But it's waiting for clear instructions. If it receives a panicked order, such as "Don't miss!" the command isn't clear. The body is only being told what *not* to do. It's much better to talk to yourself in the affirmative. Instead of "Don't miss!" calmly say to yourself, "Just put the ball in the basket."

In a recent edition of *Coaching Management*, Geno Auriemma, women's coach at University of Connecticut, said it was important to get the players to "expect to make every shot. Sometimes you need to notice how you phrase a thought. Instead of saying 'If we keep missing free throws, we're going to lose,' it may work better to say, 'We're going to work on free throw shooting and let's make every one.' Now the focus is on making shots as opposed to missing them."

Expectations are vitally important. I was talking to a coach the other day and he suggested that Michael Jordan was such a high scorer because "every time he shoots, he expects to make the basket. Every single time."

COACHING THE MIND

While most players know the mental game is important, they have no idea how to control their minds. It's easier to work on mechanics—passing, dribbling, layups. We can usually *see* when something is going wrong. Cause and effect exist in the physical world. But when it comes to the mental game, there's no way we can look in our heads to see what's going wrong.

I'm not a psychologist or a psychiatrist—although I talked to many of them while searching for my free throw method—and I'm not going to get into a lot of fancy theories. But I do know one thing for sure: If you want to sink a free throw under pressure, you have to be in control of your mind, in the same way you have learned to control your muscles.

When I talk about controlling your mind, what I'm really saying is you can't let it get in your way. You have to keep it busy—or better yet, keep it clear—while the body does what it's been trained to do. The job, then, is to use your mind, to empty your mind for the brief period of time just before and while you are shooting a free throw.

Players often ask me what is the best state of mind to be in when shooting free throws. I like to turn the question around on them. "What's the abbreviation for mountain?" I ask. Then I point to my head. "MT—empty."

It's kind of a corny joke, but it helps them remember this important point. Maybe you should tap yourself on the forehead just before shooting and repeat the word *empty*. That motion could be a trigger to clear your mind.

An excellent way to achieve this state of emptiness, in which focus and concentration come naturally, is by using a *mantra*.

A FREE THROW MANTRA

Zen masters, who can send an arrow into a bull's-eye in a darkened room, know more about concentration than I ever will. So I have adopted their use of a mantra to achieve a quiet state of mind at the free throw line.

A mantra is often used to describe a word or phrase that is repeated over and over for reassurance. This is true. But it's not the whole meaning of mantra.

While meditating, a person repeats a mantra until his or her mind reaches a state of emptiness. The mantra keeps the mind busy; it becomes that one conscious thought the mind is capable of at a single moment. This state allows the natural self to function more freely.

It is in this state of empty mind that basketball players hit a three-pointer while off balance and twisted around a point guard. It is in this state of mind that a tennis player returns a seemingly impossible passing shot at the net or a shortstop dives to catch a screaming line drive.

I once saw the great tennis player Pete Sampras interviewed after winning a major tournament. The interviewer asked what he was thinking during his spectacular performance. His answer was elegantly simple: "Nothing." He wasn't being glib or uncooperative. He was honestly describing the mental zone that top athletes play in. Some athletes have said that being in the zone is like watching someone else play. They give complete control of their bodies to their reflexes and to muscle memory. The mind sits back and enjoys the show.

We can find this quiet mind while in times of intense action under the hoop. It's much harder to find it at the free throw line with too much time to think. But with this mantra, you can empty the mind and let the body do what it has done thousands of times in practice.

Instead of engaging in self-destructive dialogues about how you're a choke artist or speculating whether you're *hot* or guessing what luck holds in store for you, focus your attention on the task at hand. You are in complete control. The basket is still 15 feet away, 10 feet above the floor. Being under pressure hasn't changed this. A crowd of screaming fans won't change the flight of the ball.

If your focus is powerful enough, you will feel that it is just you, the basket, and the ball. All working together.

Remember your ritual. This is where you need it. Repeat the steps to yourself. As you hear the mantra, you will feel reassured, relaxed. And it will evoke the memory of all those free throws you've successfully sunk in practice.

Feet square to the line. Bounce the ball three times. Thumb in the channel. Elbow in. Bend the knees. Eye on the target. Shoot and follow through.

THE "INNER" GAME

The mental game can be played in a number of ways. W. Timothy Gallwey has written extensively about the "inner" games of tennis, golf, and skiing. What he has discovered is something I think all serious athletes should consider.

When he was a teenager, Gallwey was closing out an opponent in a national junior tennis tournament when he hit an easy volley into the net. He began to ask himself why he missed the absurdly easy shot—and his search for the answer to this question spanned many years and launched his career as an author and lecturer.

Gallwey concluded that as we play sports, our minds are divided as if there are two people or "selves" with different personalities. One is analytical, overly judgmental and ultimately inhibiting. He called this side "Self One." The other side of your mind is quiet, confident, and filled with amazing potential. This is "Self Two." When playing sports, Self One is constantly judging, criticizing, and attempting to control Self Two. This becomes obvious when you hear a player yelling at him or herself, "You fool! How'd you miss that shot? You were wide open!"

Gallwey's solution to this was, first of all, to recognize

this split nature of the mind and, second, to learn to trust Self Two. To accomplish this he employed a technique that is similar to the use of a mantra. In tennis, when the ball is approaching, you watch until the ball hits the court. When you see this you say, in your head, "Bounce." Then, as you swing the racket, you say "Hit" at the moment you actually stroke the ball.

The purpose of this "bounce, hit" technique, is to keep the conscious mind, Self One, busy while Self Two accomplishes the task. It's like sending the boss out on a pointless errand so the workers can stay behind and get the job done.

If I were to compare my technique to Gallwey's "bounce, hit," I would say that the act of looking for the inflation hole and silently repeating the mantra accomplishes the same end. The conscious mind, which interferes in situations such as at the free throw line, is tied up in the meaningless visual act of looking for the inflation hole.

PROCESS, *NOT* RESULTS

A friend of mine, Dr. James Jen Kin, is one of the country's top boxing referees, a martial arts expert, and a renowned sports psychiatrist. I knew my method worked, because I had used it successfully many times. But I was interested in hearing what an expert would say about it. After hearing me describe my free throw shooting method, he said that when athletes get under pressure they become fixated on *results*. At the free throw line this would, of course, mean making two baskets.

If you could read the basketball player's mind, he or she might be saying, "I've *got* to make this basket! If I don't we'll lose the game. If I lose this game we'll blow the championship. If we lose the championship . . ." Instead, Dr. Jen

Kin said that the player in the pressure-packed situation should be thinking, "Okay, start the process. Remember all the steps. Do them all just right and the ball will go in the basket."

When an athlete focuses on the process, Dr. Jen Kin said, the results will take care of themselves. "You could almost say to yourself, 'I'm going to do everything just right and the hell with the results.'"

MY FOCUS IS CHALLENGED

My ability to concentrate was challenged by TV reporter Rick Lozano on ABC's *World News Tonight*. He apparently didn't believe I was serious when I said I could block everything else out of my mind. He told me to go ahead and shoot a few free throws. Then, without warning, he jumped at me, shouting and waving his arms, trying to distract me. I still didn't miss.

Oddly enough, I have to say I didn't even notice him. Or maybe I noticed him with another part of my consciousness. I was aware that he was there, and that he was moving toward me. But I had decided beforehand that I was going to make the free throw. I was into my ritual, and all I heard was the mantra I was repeating in my head. That one thought was powerful enough to block everything else from my mind.

That experience taught me the value of the ritual. It showed that the pieces of my process are linked together so that, once it is started, it continues despite distractions. My focus moves from the inflation hole to my target, without interruption. It's like my focus is following a chain of events that always leads to the basket.

If you are a free throw shooter standing at the line in a tight game, you know the crowd behind the basket is going to be shouting and waving their arms, trying to get you to miss. This observation should be filed in your mind before starting the process. Decide ahead of time you won't let it throw you off. Remind yourself that the process will put you into a state of auto-hypnosis. The crowd can scream themselves hoarse and it won't keep your shot from finding the basket.

A CONSTANT CHALLENGE

The players I've coached come back to me and say, "If I just focus and concentrate I can make my free throws. The ones I miss are the ones where my mind wanders." Building your powers of concentration—learning to focus and concentrate—is something you have to work on with as much determination as your shooting mechanics. It starts with understanding the difference between how your mind works when you are flying down the court on a fast break and how it works when you're standing on the free throw line getting ready to shoot two for your team's victory.

Let me come full circle now and sum up this chapter.

Once you have mastered the mechanics of free throw shooting, you have to do two things. The first is to adopt a generally positive outlook, free of self-defeating negative thoughts. Then you have to develop a way to control your thoughts by achieving a state of focus and concentration. Never let your mind wander away where it might find something in the past or future that will suddenly flash onto the screen of your mind. If this happens, it creates tension in the body that results in a missed shot. Instead, keep your mind in the here and now by repeating the mantra and keeping your eyes focused on the inflation hole. Begin your ritual, free the muscle memory, let your body take over. And the ball will go into the basket.

Let focus and concentration work for you, just as it has for me. When someone asks me to autograph their basketball, I always write the two words that I think are most important to accomplish any task: "Focus and concentrate, Tom Amberry."

essential member of the team. Height, strength, and speed are of no advantage when you're standing on the line.

In the last two chapters we looked at mechanics and the mental side of free throw shooting. Now I'm going to combine those two elements of free throw shooting and see how they work together under game conditions. We're going to take two free throws and watch them in slow motion. I hope that as you read this, you will *live* this scenario. Feel it. Experience it. Then, when you are faced with the same situation in a game, it will be a familiar, comfortable, blended series of movements.

DEALING WITH ANGER

The free throw shooting process often begins when you pick yourself up off the floor. You've been decked by a point guard or hacked by a power forward. Physical contact (and especially pain) brings anger and a desire to retaliate. Well, you'd better deal with your emotions before you go to the line. Your anger won't help you there.

I'm not telling you how to play the game. If you want to settle the score in some way, that's up to you. But the first order of business is to sink your free throws. How do you clear your head before shooting? Although it's difficult to eliminate anger, it's easy to postpone it. Tell yourself, "After I make these two free throws I'll deal with that —" (you finish the sentence). Then, after you hit the back of the net twice and go back to pick up your anger, you may find it's not there anymore. The free throws were enough of a revenge.

This is an important lesson for free throw shooting, and for life. If you try to repress or cancel an emotion, that feeling seems to become even stronger. But before you lash out, try stalling the emotion. As a boy, I was taught to count to ten before I said something in anger. Later, I forced myself

4

Put Yourself on the Line

Shooting is a con game. Confidence. Concentration. Control. Consistency. Conditioning.

SHOOTING COACH ERNIE HOBBIE

My purpose in writing this book is not to tell you how to make hundreds of free throws in a row. I want to tell you how to make just two free throws in a row, when you really need to. That's what free throw shooting is all about.

Let's face it, making a long string of free throws is boring to everyone except the person who is doing the shooting. When I put on clinics, I make 25 in a row just to show I can do it. My audience usually watches the first 10 free throws with a great deal of interest. Then they talk through the rest of my shooting. But by the end of it they are convinced I know what I'm doing.

Free throws are most exciting within the context of the game of basketball. The rule was created to make the game as a whole work. But it's also a chance for a player to show off a different set of skills: concentration, discipline, and control. And it's an opportunity for any player—maybe even the guy who's been warming the bench all year—to be an to "sleep on it" before picking up the phone and giving someone a piece of my mind. Usually, I found that putting time between the initial anger and possible retaliation gave my hot emotions time to cool down, or even disappear.

Okay, your emotions are—at least temporarily—under control. Then what?

GETTING READY

If you are fouled in the final seconds of the game, the opposing coach is likely to call a time-out to "ice" you before you go to the line. Even if that doesn't occur, there is always a brief waiting period before you shoot your free throws. This is the danger zone for a free throw shooter. It's during these seconds that negative thoughts can accumulate and the pressure builds to a point where it disrupts your ability to make a simple shot.

When a concept is expressed in a catchy phrase, such as "icing a player," it can lodge in your mind. If you know the other team is trying to ice you, having that thought in your mind will be harmful. So turn their words around on them. Reverse the strategy. Tell yourself you have "ice water" in your veins—you are so cool under pressure no amount of time can keep you from making the free throws.

In the 1954 All-Star Game in Madison Square Garden, George Mikan was fouled as the final buzzer ended the game. Mikan had to make both free throws for the West team to survive. The East's coach had two time-outs left—and called them both. A total of five minutes passed before Mikan was handed the ball. He calmly sank the first free throw. Then he stepped away, took a deep breath, and put the second shot cleanly through the net to force an overtime period. Mikan demonstrated that it is possible to overcome a delay, even an extremely long one.

Stalling will affect you only if you let it. Make sure, during this period of time, that you don't let doubts grow. If negative thoughts invade your mind, don't struggle to repress them. This usually starts a losing battle. Instead, realize that no matter what thoughts are going through your head now, you already know what to do when you shoot your free throws. That's the value of the seven-step process. You know what your body—and your mind—has to do. Feel confident because you have a secret weapon.

USING IMAGES TO REMOVE DOUBT

If your mind begins playing pictures of the ball bouncing off the rim and missing the basket, you need to deal with those images before you shoot. There are two ways that our thinking process works. We talk to ourselves (not out loud, I hope) and we also think in pictures. These pictures are especially powerful in programming future performance. If negative images invade your mind at this crucial moment, take a moment, before beginning your ritual, to flash a sure-fire image on the movie screen of your mind.

Picture yourself standing on the line holding the ball. As you shoot, see your arm reaching out until it's 15 feet long. Now drop the ball softly into the basket. As I mentioned earlier, this image was given to me by Coach Strain, a sports psychologist. When I first started using it I noticed an immediate decrease in my anxiety level at the free throw line. And it can work for you, too. Let this simple picture replace the negative scenes you've imagined and remove all doubt from your mind. You will now feel that putting the ball in the basket is as easy as putting a spoonful of your favorite dessert into your mouth.

PLAY THE ODDS

If this type of imagery is too far-out for you, there is still one more strategy that works. Put your trust in the facts. If you have been regularly practicing free throw shooting, you can remind yourself of your average. Maybe you're shooting 90 percent in practice. Tell yourself you have a nine-to-one chance of putting the ball in the net. The chances of a 90 percent free throw shooter missing two in a row are one in one hundred. Those are strong odds. Let them work in your favor by giving you a mental boost.

Finally, here are a few practical steps to use as you get ready to take your free throws:

Train yourself to have confident thoughts as soon as you're fouled. These thoughts should be simple, direct and realistic, such as, "I can do it." Or, "No problem. Just put the ball in the basket." Allow panicked, negative instructions, such as "I can't miss!" to drop from your mind.

Walk slowly to the line to begin the deliberate—but relaxed—rhythm that promotes good free throw shooting. This is especially important if you are winded. Take advantage of the ten-second rule to catch your breath.

If you are perspiring heavily, get a towel and dry your hands. Good free throw shooting means having a good sense of touch.

Keep your legs loose by doing some deep knee bends. You will need a smooth push from your legs to give proper distance.

Concentrate on breathing deeply and evenly to reduce tension.

Get in position at the line only when you're ready to shoot. Standing at the line before the shot brings feelings of pressure. Step to the line to begin your ritual.

Don't stare at the hoop. You know where it is. Aside from

that, sighting the target is part of your ritual and that comes later.

POINTS OF FOCUS

The ref hands you the ball now, and the moment of truth is approaching. The crowd noise is probably swelling. The tension is growing thick around you. This is when you need to go into your mental routine. You need to find that quiet inner place where you can concentrate. This is also when you need to control your point of focus.

It is at this crucial moment that all the hours of practice pay off. You have worked hard for just this situation. And you know exactly how to respond. You are about to show yourself, your team, your coach and the crowd the depth of your character. You will show them all that you are mentally strong.

Don't look at the scoreboard, or your teammates, or your opponents. Don't stare at the basket. Turn the ball so the inflation hole is looking up at you. Step to the line and slowly bounce the ball three times, keeping your eye on the inflation hole. As you do this something wonderful will happen. The inflation hole, and the three slow bounces, will trigger a powerful association. It will remind you of all the times in practice you did the exact same thing. And in practice, the ball almost always went through the net.

You suddenly feel grounded, "centered," back on familiar ground. You know exactly what to do, and what will happen next. What we are really talking about here is muscle memory. Your mind has told your body, "Do what you have done a thousand times before."

When you catch the ball after the final bounce, you put your thumb in the groove and your fingers spread out over the ball. This is the way you hold the ball every time you shoot your free throws. It continues that feeling of familiarity the previous steps have started.

With the ball in your hands, your eyes are still on the inflation hole. Now, like a powerful beam of light, or like the lens on a camera, your eyes go directly from the inflation hole to the space above the back rim of the basket. As you do this the ball is raised into the shooting position just below your chin. You are now sighting over the top of the ball at the basket.

Let me interrupt this description for a moment to stress something vitally important. It is at this moment that many players freeze. Naturally, they want to make absolutely sure this shot goes in. To accomplish that goal they take an extra moment to "make sure" by staring at the target. This is actually counterproductive because it results in a condition called "focal dystonia."

Focal dystonia is a fancy way of saying that when you stare at something for a long time, the image fades. You can still see what you are looking at, but its image in your brain is no longer vivid. This is the last thing you want to happen to your target. So you need to shoot while that first flash of the target is blazing in your mind.

There is another important concept at work here. I've spoken repeatedly about bypassing the thinking process of the mind. One way to do this is not to give the mind time to engage its rational qualities.

Police officers are given handgun training by flashing a sudden target in front of them. They don't have time to raise their weapon, sight along the barrel and fire. The aiming has to be instinct. Use that same principle here. In game action you are used to shooting without staring at the target. Do the same thing now.

Let's start the film again and watch the rest of the free throw. With your eyes on the target and the ball in the shooting position, you bend your knees. As I said before, the knee bend initiates the final steps of the process. From here on, the shot should sweep smoothly up through your body like a wave. But let me remind you what those motions are.

As you bend your knees your elbow comes into the "shot pocket." As your legs straighten, the arm takes over and extends straight at the basket. These two motions are closely linked and beyond your conscious control. So don't try to control them. Don't guide the basketball. Shoot it. You have the feeling of reaching out toward the basket, as if to drape your hand over the front rim of the basket. You are vaguely conscious of your wrist snapping down and feel the ball rolling off your fingertips.

Remember that you have trained yourself not to watch the ball in flight. Instead, your eyes remain comfortably fixed on the space above the basket. A moment later, the ball drops through this target area. And you hear the crowd roar as the ball hits the net.

You might now have a feeling of coming out of a deep state of concentration. That's fine. You don't need to concentrate right now. But you will in a few seconds because you have to shoot another free throw.

SHOOTING THE SECOND FREE THROW

Let's say the first free throw went through the hoop but was not picture perfect. Maybe it hit the front rim but dropped in. Or maybe it was off line a bit and rattled around before it finally dropped in. Not only does this make your heart skip a beat (and adds good drama for the crowd), but it also tells you what to do on your next shot.

Never say to yourself, "You almost missed it short. Shoot this one longer!" Don't compare your next shot to your previous one. That shot is history. It's gone. But you can learn from it.

What you need to do is always strive for the perfect free throw, the one that finds the center of the basket. Go back to that concept as you prepare for the second shot. This is how you do that.

If your first shot hit the front rim, remind yourself to make a deep knee bend. Don't make a *deeper* knee bend. Make the right knee bend. If the shot was off line to the right or left, remind yourself to get the elbow in and let your shooting arm go straight at the target.

With these few adjustments your second shot is up and lands dead center in the basket.

The value of my method is that the more pressure you are under, the better it works. The seven steps may seem like a lot to do in practice, when missing the shot carries no penalty. But if you have the hopes of your team and hard work of an entire season riding on one shot, doing the seven steps just right can virtually guarantee you a basket.

POSITIVE REINFORCEMENT

Let's continue this exercise for just a moment longer so we can examine the positive effects of free throw shooting. After you make the second basket, your team high-fives you and you all run back to your end of the court. Notice that there was no need to rebound. No chance for them to grab the ball and pull a fast break. You followed through on the opportunity you were given.

Now the game continues. Think about how the other team feels. You just answered their foul by converting it into points. Will they foul you again? Maybe. But soon they will realize that this is a losing strategy. Then they will have to let you shoot from the floor.

What frame of mind are you in now? Confident? Of course. You just put two more points under your name on the score sheet. Maybe those two points put you in double figures. But you also showed yourself, your team, your coach, and the crowd that your game is complete. Think about what this is worth to you and your basketball career. Keep that question in your mind as you read the next chapter on practicing free throws.

5

Perfect Practice

Magic Johnson is more workmanlike than his Showtime reputation might suggest. How many kids know that he was an above-average 78.5 percent free throw shooter as a freshman at Michigan State and then worked his way up to 91.1 percent by his 10th season in the pros. Asked how he did it, Magic had a simple response: "150 shots a day."

Sports Illustrated

It has been said that "great free throw shooters are born, not made." I completely disagree. In fact, I think this must have been said by a lazy basketball player who was looking for an excuse for his poor free throw shooting.

I believe you *can* make yourself a good free throw shooter.

Bill Sharman, an outstanding basketball player and later a terrific coach, was one of the greatest free throw shooters of all time. In his book, *Sharman on Basketball*, he writes: "Although I always felt I was a little above average in the ability to shoot free throws in high school and in my first two years at college, it wasn't until my junior year at USC that I really felt a sense of pride and dedication in improving this skill to the very highest degree possible." Here is a player who, by his own admission, was only "a little above average." His junior year at USC he went all twelve league games without missing a single free throw. In the pros, Sharman set many free throw records, including a .932 average for the '58–'59 season and a career average of .883.

Using Sharman as an example, if you consider yourself a little above average, or even average, just think what you can accomplish by practicing.

Even the word *practice* might bring an automatic resistance from some players. I know that a lot of basketball players say that practicing free throws is boring. I think that's for two reasons:

1. Most players don't know how to practice free throw shooting.
2. Players often don't see results from practicing free throws.

But what if I could guarantee that your practice quickly brought you results you could clearly measure? For example, what if, in one week, you went from making 60 out of 100 free throws to making 90 out of 100? Would you find practice boring then? I doubt it. And furthermore, what if I could guarantee that those results in practice transferred into added points in games? Then you would realize there was a definite benefit to practice. Seeing your improvement would motivate you to continue to practice, or to practice even harder.

In any sport, there is no better feeling than knowing you are improving. So your practice should be built around setting goals and measuring your improvement. As you improve, your motivation will rise.

How much can you look forward to improving? And how quickly can you implement my free throw shooting method? I think you will be amazed. In fact, if you are looking for a way to boost your game scoring average (and who isn't?), the free throw line is the best place to find those extra points.

FREE THROW REPORT CARDS

This summer I gave a free throw shooting clinic at Bob Gottlieb's Branch West Basketball Academy, in Orange County, California. I worked one-on-one for about fifteen minutes with each of the players, who ranged in age from ten to twenty-five years old. Some of the players were just starting out. Others were extremely accomplished. One player, a high school senior, was one of the top recruits for college. The players I coached all started as "average" free throw shooters—about 60 percent. I showed them the proper mechanics, taught them to focus and concentrate, then told them to shoot 100 free throws a day.

One week later I returned to the academy and they handed me "report cards," signed by their parents. I didn't tell them to document their results. They did it on their own, shooting 100 free throws a day, as I recommended. Their results amazed even me. It also reinforced my belief that, done correctly, practice brings results.

FIRST WEEK RESULTS

FIRST WEEK RESULTS

Player's Age	Mon.	Tues.	Wed.	Thurs.	Fri.	Sat.	Avg.
16	88%	92%	91%	92%	94%	91%	91%
15	81%	83%	90%	92%	85%	n/a	86%
15	70%	63%	80%	80%	81%	n/a	74%
12	72%	65%	74%	75%	73%	74%	72%

Do you think that these kids found practicing boring? They were walking a foot above the floor. And they promised they would keep practicing and improving.

MUSCLE MEMORY

Practice is the time to try new moves. And it's also the time to groove those moves that you've learned but may not have completely mastered. In other words, practice is the time to become comfortable with new styles of shooting and playing. In most cases, practice is a relaxed, penalty-free atmosphere. This is both good and bad. What makes free throw shooting difficult is the penalty that a missed shot carries. Therefore, as I'll show you later, you have to put as much pressure on yourself as possible to simulate game conditions. You can practice handling pressure. Continue to challenge yourself and each success will make you stronger.

What I'm really saying is that practice is the best way to build muscle memory. Most athletes are familiar with the term "muscle memory." We hear it thrown around continually. But what does it really mean? Is there really such a thing as muscle memory? And how do you develop it?

When I was in podiatry school, we were taught "Davis's Law" which was an accepted principle of physiology. Davis's Law stated that by repeating the same motion over and over again, your muscles *physically* change to carry out that action. This is good news for free throw shooters.

As I mentioned earlier, when you shoot a free throw, you are always *exactly* 15 feet from the hoop, which is *exactly* 10 feet above the boards. The basketball is always the same weight. Nothing has changed. If Davis's Law is true, and you have shot your 100 free throws during every practice session, then you really will have "muscle memory." If you can clear your mind of pressure, your body will sink the shot. The memory of how to shoot the free throw will live in your muscles as well as your mind.

DOES PRACTICE MAKE PERFECT?

Since you are training your muscles to remember how to shoot free throws, it is essential that you do everything correctly in practice. That's why I believe the old expression "Practice makes perfect" is only partly true. You can practice all you like, but if your methods are flawed, you won't get any better. Instead, you will imprint harmful patterns more deeply. This is why I prefer the expression "Perfect practice makes perfect."

Every time you practice free throws, make sure all your mechanics are perfect. If necessary, begin by reviewing the seven steps in Chapter 2. Then, when warming up, don't go to the line cold. Shoot your way to the line. Starting only a foot or two from the basket, be sure you sink the very first shot you take. Then step back and shoot again. You don't have to do the seven steps, but use good shooting technique—square up, elbow in, bend the knees, eye on the target. Finally, start shooting from the line using the seven steps. Each shot will take you only six seconds. With a few seconds to retrieve the ball, you will quickly reach your goal of 100.

Whenever you miss, ask yourself whether it was caused by improper mechanics or a lack of focus. If you still have trouble finding the problem, look at Chapter 6 on troubleshooting.

One of the challenges facing you in practice is to stay focused. Since there is no pressure, it's harder to focus. Your mind will wander—if you let it. That's why it's so important to keep score.

SET UP A DAILY ROUTINE

I shoot 500 free throws a day. If I have to skip a practice session because I'm traveling, I'm not as good the next day. So I've come to accept the fact that practice is like filling up a leaky bucket—you have to do it every day to stay sharp.

My recommendation for most high school and college players is to shoot 100 free throws a day. Does this sound unrealistic? Then I have to ask you: How good do you want to be? Anyone serious about improving their free throw shooting—and their game—will take the time to practice. Remember Magic Johnson and his 150 free throws a day. During the game he is a showman, but he puts in his time at the line in practice.

If you practice, and stay focused for the entire time, your efforts should result in a 90 percent free throw average in games. If you want a higher game average, you may have to shoot more free throws each day.

It will help you stick with your routine if you practice at the same time and place everyday. If you're on a team, get to the gym early and shoot before practice. If that's not possible, stay after practice. You can also shoot at home in your driveway or at the neighborhood courts, but outdoor shooting is more difficult. And in the winter, depending on where you live, it may be impossible.

KEEPING SCORE

One essential aspect of free throw practice is to keep score. Keeping track of your results will document your improvement. As you see yourself improving, it will motivate you to work harder and concentrate more deeply.

When you are starting out, shoot your 100 free throws in sets of 10. After 10, step away from the line and write down how many you made. Your goal, of course, is to make all 10. Then, when you go back to the line, bear down and make that first one of the new set. Now you've got a streak going.

As you improve, and your sets of 10 include fewer misses, you may not need to write down the results. All you need to know is how many sets you've done. For some reason it's easy to lose track of how many free throws you've shot. (I have heard it said that being "in the zone" draws heavily on the right side of the brain, which is nonmathematical. Maybe losing track of the score means you're concentrating deeply.)

To keep track of the number of sets you've shot, try this. If you're wearing shorts or athletic warm-ups that have pockets, put 10 pennies in your right pocket. When you finish shooting 10 free throws, move one penny into your left pocket. When all the pennies are in your left pocket, you're done with practice.

Once it becomes routine for you to make 10 out of 10 (and believe me, it will) then shoot in increments of 20, then four groups of 25. If you get to the level of making all 25 free throws, you are in a very select group. The next goal will be 50, and then 100.

Using a free throw shooting notebook is a good way to break up the process. You may also begin to see trends you would otherwise miss. For example, I've noticed that I have my best shooting days on Mondays. I used to laugh at the idea of biorhythms, but maybe there is something to it. The notebook will become like a contract between you and yourself. It shows you your performance and proves your dedication to improvement.

COACHING FREE THROWS

I talk to a lot of coaches, and I know how frustrated they are with their players' free throw shooting performances. I can't say I've ever met a coach who didn't feel there was room for improvement on the free throw line. Every coach seems to have an immediate example at hand where free throw shooting cost them a game or a championship. But recall Jerry Tarkanian's admission that "very few coaches really know how to teach free throw shooting."

I recommend that coaches become completely familiar with my method of free throw shooting before they present it to their team. This means using the steps to shoot until you believe it really works. You have to believe in what you are preaching. Your excitement and conviction will come through in many small ways, and your belief will come from first-hand experience. Much of coaching is trying to communicate a *feeling*. How can you describe the feeling unless you've experienced it?

When working one-on-one with your players, your trained eye can provide valuable feedback to someone trying to master the technique. Maybe a player thinks his or her elbow is tucked in. But you, standing behind, can see it is still waving in the breeze. In addition to working on mechanics, work on self-image. Motivate players in positive ways. Let them know you believe in them and their skill. Reassure them that you don't expect instant perfection. But at the same time require them to commit to change and growth.

Remember that players can only learn a certain amount at one time before they begin to feel lost. Each basketball player has a sense of personal style that he or she is probably proud of. Let it be known that you will not change that style anywhere except at the free throw line. Then, as you teach my method, begin by enforcing the main points first. I would say you should focus on squaring up, bending the knees, and bringing the elbow in. Don't immediately require them to do all the other steps perfectly.

A SYSTEMATIC APPROACH

One of the biggest problems with changing a player's free throw shooting style is that he or she will revert to old habits under pressure. That's because when players are under the gun, they tend to seek the familiar—even if it hasn't been very successful for them. What you as a coach can do is design and implement a free throw shooting program that has a chance to permanently improve your team. If you are reading this at the beginning of a season, you are in a position to make some radical changes to the free throw styles used by your players. By the time the season begins, they will have become comfortable with their new style and confident enough to use it under pressure.

If you are reading this in midseason, you might want to select only those players with the very lowest free throw shooting averages to work with. One sad fact is that some of the best players have the lowest free throw shooting averages. A player who is excellent in every other way becomes a liability when are fouled in the final seconds of a close game.

Coaches may have players on their teams who are already good free throw shooters. It may be beneficial to set a certain cutoff point above which you won't require them to change. If players are shooting above, say, 80 percent, they will not be required to change their free throw shooting style. Players below, perhaps, 60 percent should be expected to adopt the seven steps.

One problem facing many coaches is that the gym may have only two or four baskets while the team has fourteen or more players. Consequently, the coach should let the players practice on their own time or arrange for them to shoot free throws before or after practice. Later in this chapter I will suggest some drills in which the whole team can participate.

Coaches also feel that there is not enough time to practice free throw shooting. There are so many other aspects of the game that have to be addressed. Aside from that, the mention of free throw shooting may bring groans of protest from the team. Tell the team that free throw shooting is a vital addition to the scoring system of a team. Add that practicing free throw shooting will increase three-point shooting skills. That will raise their interest level instantly.

During practice, the coach should stop the scrimmage and take the whole team to the line for free throws. This is particularly important toward the end of practice when the players are getting tired. Try to put as much pressure as possible on the players. Make sure the whole team is watching the shooter. Explain to them that you are simulating game conditions. If the players can learn to handle pressure in practice, it will boost their confidence. Eventually they will learn to cope more successfully with pressure in the games.

Set up a performance chart and post it where all the players can see it. Offer rewards for the highest free throw percentage in individual practice, in team practice and in the games. A separate reward could be offered for the player with the longest free throw shooting streak. In this way, you can have several players with top honors. Motivate your team using a variety of goals and incentives.

Another area where the coach can make a vast difference is in creating a mental climate of pride surrounding free throw shooting. Don't participate in self-deprecatory humor, even if you haven't won a game. Urge the players to think of themselves as excellent free throw shooters—or at least a team that is working hard to improve. The players should be encouraged to think of themselves as being tough under pressure. If you can motivate them to improve, and boost their self-image, their performance will surpass anything you could ever imagine. And it could turn a losing season into a winning year.

DRILLS FOR SKILLS

One of the best ways to motivate players to improve their free throw shooting is to give each player on your team a free throw shooting partner. Match a strong shooter with a weak one so they can needle each other into getting better. Then, toward the end of practice, when the team is tired and wants to hit the showers, have these free throw shooting teams spread out evenly at the baskets and challenge each other. The players rotate so that each one takes two shots. The first pair that makes 30 free throws gets to leave. The losers then face each other and shoot 20. Soon only two teams are left.

This drill works for a number of reasons. It puts pressure on the players. It simulates game conditions by having one player penalized by a partner's poor performance. Finally, it rewards the best players and penalizes the worst. You may find that the players who chronically lose will put in extra time on their own to improve their skills.

Here is a variation on the same drill. Again, following a hard scrimmage, tell the players to spread out evenly at all the baskets. Have each player shoot until he or she makes five in a row or misses. The other players are instructed to rebound for the missed shots.

This drill encourages the players to make every free throw for two reasons. Most athletes have the natural inclination to remain in the spotlight as long as possible. In this drill they can do that—as long as they don't miss. Also, if the players are tired, they would rather be shooting free throws than rebounding.

A free throw shooting ladder is a good way to develop interest in free throw shooting and motivate your players to spend extra time practicing. Some members of your team who see little action during the game have a chance to excel and maybe even exceed the ability of the better players. Post the ladder in a prominent place in the locker room, or in your office, and give the players a way to challenge those above them on the ladder. You could even create some time once a week where the team can have shoot-offs and announce the results.

Ron Herrin, assistant men's coach at Southern Illinois University, awards T-shirts to players based on how many consecutive free throws they can make. Making 25 in a row gets them a T-shirt with "Club 25" on it, 50 in a row puts them in "Club 50" and 100 in a row gets them a polo shirt with "Century Club" written on it. I think this is a good way to motivate the players to develop their free throw shooting skills and take pride in their accomplishments.

If you and your team are serious about improving at the

line you should run one drill each practice that improves free throw shooting. Vary the drills I've described above, or invent your own. But get the players used to the fact that free throw shooting is an important part of basketball, and that it is something that you, as a coach, will help them improve at.

Finally, I think it is an excellent idea for you to encourage your players to set a personal goal for free throw shooting. Tell them to pick a specific average they hope to achieve in practice and in the games. (It is generally thought that the average in the game will be about 5 percent lower than in practice; the difference in performance is due to the pressure the player faces.) When setting the goal, the player should also include how much practice he or she intends to do every day to achieve this level. In the next chapter, I have talked in more detail about goal setting.

You could also discuss setting a free throw shooting goal as a team. Bear in mind that the free throw shooting average of a team is usually close to its win-loss average. In other words, if you set a high goal for free throw shooting, you are really setting a goal to win most of your games.

There is, however, another goal you could consider setting—one that would bring an enormous amount of recognition to your team. Few teams have made all their free throws in one game. If your players all individually raise their free throw shooting averages, the team as a whole could achieve this rare accomplishment.

SHOOTING IN YOUR HEAD

When you can't get to the gym to practice, you can't improve your free throw shooting. Right? Wrong. Just thinking about free throw shooting will improve your on-the-court performance.

The benefit of "mental practice" was clearly proved in an amazing study by the researcher Dr. Alvaro Pascual-Leone, a neurologist at the Universidad De Valencia, in Valencia, Spain. Dr. Pascual-Leone wanted to study how humans practice and learn to perform athletic activities. He used free throw shooting to prove his point.

Dr. Pascual-Leone set up three groups with ten volunteers in each group. These were "ordinary people," not basketball players.

The first group didn't touch a basketball at all. Their only activity was to *visualize* shooting and scoring free throws. They did this for one hour a day. The second group didn't perform any visualization. Instead, they did what most basketball players do—they shot free throws. They did this for one hour a day. The third group combined the activities of the first two groups. In other words, the people in this group *physically* shot free throws for forty-five minutes, and *visualized* shooting free throws for fifteen minutes.

At the end of five days, the three groups were called together and each person shot 20 free throws. Group one, which only visualized shooting, made the fewest number of free throws. The second group, which practiced physically, made substantially more free throws. But the group that practiced both physically and mentally made the most free throws.

"Anything that can be improved with physical practice may be benefited by mental practice," Dr. Pascual-Leone said. "This is important since physical practice is not always possible. If an injured athlete continues to practice mentally while the injury heals, he or she may prevent some loss of skill."

There is a mind-blowing principle at work here. Basically, Dr. Pascual-Leone is saying that when we vividly imagine doing something, our bodies think we really are doing it.

Have you ever been on the edge of sleep, thinking about basketball practice maybe, and suddenly seen a ball coming right at your head? What do you do? You duck. Right there in bed. That's because you thought the ball was real.

If you create a scene in which you are going to the line with a big game at stake, your body will think it's real. You will feel nervous, your muscles will tense. But you can completely control the outcome of this imaginary scene.

Take a few moments before you go to sleep at night, or just before a big game, to stroke a few free throws—in your head. Picture yourself being nervous but in control. Rehearse the seven steps. Shoot the ball and always, always, always, see the ball find the net. Then, when your big moment comes, you already know what's going to happen.

A PERFECT ENDING

Finally, I would like to offer one more piece of advice about practice. Whenever possible, never quit on a miss. Make sure the very last free throw is a perfect swish. Shoot until you get everything right—good follow-through, nice arc, all net—then pick up your ball and go home. That last basket will be stamped in your memory. It will give you a positive self-image to dwell on. Let that perfect free throw live in your body and your mind until you come out to play or practice again.

6

Troubleshooting

You've been running a 100-yard dash, and then you're asked to play six bars on the piano of a concerto by some great composer.

UConn Coach Jim Calhoun on free throw shooting

In the second game of the 1995 NBA Western Conference semifinals between the Lakers and the Spurs, Vlade Divac went to the line with 4.6 seconds on the clock and the score tied at 83. He had two chances to claim victory for his team. It was the most important free throw situation of his life.

His first shot hit the front of the rim and fell short.

Both benches and the 26,127 spectators in the Alamodome stood as Divac raised the ball for his second shot. The ball arced through the air, hit the back of the rim and bounced out.

The first shot was short—the second was long. This is a common mistake for players trying to troubleshoot their free throw shot under pressure. Obviously, this indicates that the shooter overadjusted.

Am I suggesting that a player should *not* change anything following a missed shot? Not at all. The worst thing in the world would be to miss short twice. But don't look for a successful future shot by comparing it to a missed shot in the past.

In a game, the emphasis shouldn't be on making "adjustments." Adjustments often mean asking the body to make too radical a change. It places too much emphasis on one part of the process. Chances are you have missed by a very small margin. You should mentally return to that perfect free throw you have sunk so many times in practice. This may mean little more than a reminder or a mental note that, once placed in your mind, will blend smoothly with the existing motion for a successful second shot.

You know what a perfect free throw looks like. You've sunk thousands of them in practice. Now go back to the perfect free throw in your mind. If you shoot thinking *make this one longer* or *make this one shorter* chances are your adjustment will be too extreme.

What exactly do you do in between free throws? First, let's look at some common shooting problems, then I'll get back to this important question.

EXPECTATIONS VS. RESULTS

When I give free throw shooting clinics and teach my seven-step method to players, I often see an enormous improvement *immediately*. This is surprising because the players may only be doing five of the seven steps correctly. They may bounce the ball twice instead of three times. Their elbows might still be out too far or their feet are staggered on the line. Still, the ball is finding the hoop.

I like to think that each one of the seven steps brings about a 14 percent improvement. If you do all the steps perfectly, practice regularly, and have a strong mental attitude, you'll make 100 percent of your free throws. But if you forget one step, your percentage drops to 86 percent; forget two steps and you're down to 72 percent. Let your mind wander and it all falls apart.

If you're merely shooting free throws to increase your percentage, 80 percent might seem good enough. But let's not forget what all this is about. As a basketball player, the day will come when you—like Vlade Divac—*absolutely, positively must make two free throws.* That's why you're reading this book. And that's why you're going to shoot 100 free throws every day of practice.

On the Soviet basketball teams of the 1970s, they practically made free throw shooting a life or death issue. When one Soviet player was shooting free throws, the rest of the team went back to the other end of the court. The message was clear. There will be no rebound because *the free throw will be in the net!* If not, the player disappeared into Siberia. Do you think this added to their motivation? I strongly suspect it did.

This concept of do-or-die was also practiced by the great golfer Ben Hogan. He once said that he concentrated on his short putts "as if someone was holding a gun to my head." I don't necessarily advocate the Soviets' or Hogan's approach. But free throws should be taken seriously. Don't set out to achieve an 80 percent free throw average. Your goal should be to make every free throw.

MISSING TO THE RIGHT AND LEFT

When you miss, you will want to know why. If you can find out why you missed, you can fix the problem. Right? Well, the difficulty with this reasoning is that you can be doing all the steps correctly but your head isn't into it. So you still miss. On the other hand, your form might be off, but your touch is just right. And you make the basket. Still, you have to analyze the physical data. Let's do that first.

Start by trying to identify a trend. Are your shots missing right or left? This is likely to be an alignment problem. Make sure your feet are square to the line and your shoulders will naturally square up, too.

With your feet square to the line you should now make sure your elbow comes in just before you start the shot. Don't hold it in an unnatural position for long periods of time. Snap it in as your knees bend. Then the initial push for the shot comes on—or close to—the center line leading to the middle of the target.

In practice I hope you have experienced that feeling of having your forearm in the "shot pocket." This gives me an enormous sense of confidence because I know, with my arm starting in the shot pocket, and extending naturally toward the back center of the rim, the ball will find the target. This simplifies the process by removing the pressure of "aiming." Bringing the elbow in is so important I sometimes tell players to rub their side raw by brushing it with their shooting elbow. Then you know your shot is starting from the right place.

There is one difficulty with trying to troubleshoot your own free throws. You may *feel* you are doing one thing when you are actually doing something very different. You may feel you're bringing your elbow in. But in reality it's still out there. Have a teammate stand behind you while you're shooting to watch your elbow.

Better yet, if you have a video camera, take some shots of your free throws. If you're hitting a high percentage, and feeling confident, watch this recorded image closely. Let it sink deep into your subconscious as an example for your mind to follow.

SHORT AND LONG SHOTS

Are your shots falling short? This is apt to happen in games because players become tentative under pressure and don't make a complete knee bend. When I really have to make a free throw, this is the one step I remind myself of before starting my routine. Here's why.

As I said before, the legs initiate the interrelated motions of the free throw. Legs first, then arm and finally wrist snap. If the legs begin by giving the right push, your body senses this and the arm is used mainly to give pinpoint accuracy. The ball has a nice high arc with plenty of rotation.

If the legs don't bend enough, then the other motions are trying to make up for that loss. The shot is pushed. The ball has too much speed, a low arc, and little rotation. If you are lucky, you make the shot anyway. But if you hit the rim, it has little chance of going in.

While a good leg bend helps raise the arc, you also have to have a sense of the arc you want. I believe this starts with the words you use to describe the shot yourself. As I mentioned earlier, think of the ball dropping through the space above the back rim of the basket. Or use Rick Barry's phrase "up to the basket." This automatically raises the arc without having to look for mechanical fixes.

In practice, concentrate on that feeling of letting the shots originate from the legs. Think of the lower half of your body being active and the arms and shoulders reacting to a motion that is already in progress. When you get your legs working properly, you will feel that your arm is doing no work at all and that aiming takes care of itself.

DEVELOPING *FEEL*

Your confidence at the line is directly related to the touch you have for shooting free throws. But your touch is difficult to retain in the games—largely because of pressure and lack of focus. The greater your touch in practice, the better your shooting will be in games. As your successes build, this will bring a greater sense of confidence which, in turn, will build your sense of touch.

Here is a way to promote fingertip control. Get an old golf glove or even a work glove. Cut the ends of the fingers off so that just the pads of your fingers stick out. Now, as you shoot free throws, pay attention to the feel of the ball as it rolls off your fingertips. Shoot a few with your eyes closed. This feeling will become magnified because there is no other way for you to get feedback. Your feel is your only indication of where the shot has gone.

As your feel improves, your release will become unhurried and smooth. Tension will cause you to "pull the string"—to cut off your release before your wrist snaps down and the ball gets the proper rotation. The more relaxed you can become at the free throw line, the greater your accuracy and control. In practice, try holding your follow-through until the ball has gone through the basket. Exaggerating this motion in practice will help ensure that you don't "pull the string" in a game.

Another way to troubleshoot your free throw is to watch how the ball behaves on shots that strike the rim. If you hit the back of the rim and it flies back at you, this means your arc is too flat. It can also mean you are not getting the proper rotation on the ball. Make sure you snap your wrist and see if those shots start to drop in. Try to get the shooter's touch.

TROUBLESHOOTING IN GAMES

The time may come when you need to troubleshoot your free throw in game conditions. Say you have missed the first free throw. It puts a tremendous pressure on your second shot because immediately you begin to see the prospect of missing both shots. This is when a tough mental attitude is required to make absolutely sure you sink the next one.

First of all, make it your rule that you will never miss two free throws in a row in a game. Why? If you're a 90 percent free throw shooter in practice, tell yourself that you now have two 9-out-of–10 chances to make a basket. The odds of missing two in a row are one in one hundred. Those are good strong odds in your favor.

What about making physical adjustments? For example, what if your first shot was short?

It's very important not to say to yourself, "I *have* to shoot this one longer." Don't look for success by comparing a future shot to a past miss. This will probably result in over-compensation and a long shot. Instead, remind yourself to make the right knee bend. Make sure you shake the tension from your legs and let the shot originate smoothly "from the ground up."

If the shot missed to the side, check your alignment. Remember to bring your elbow in. Keep your eye on the target, and don't follow the ball in flight with your eyes.

If the shot missed long, review in your mind how you picture the flight of the ball. See a high shot with just the right rotation. Relax and let your follow-through make the ball land softly.

TROUBLESHOOTING YOUR MENTAL GAME

Once you have dealt with the physical side of a missed free throw, you must look inside yourself and make sure your mind is not tripping you up.

Between the first free throw and the second, don't let negative thoughts build. If you missed the first free throw, let it drop away into the past. Get it out of your memory and your mind's eye. It's gone, it's over. You can't change it. Instead, train your sights on the next free throw.

If a negative statement jumps into your consciousness like, "What if I miss both shots?" don't try to repress it. Instead, replace it. Adopt a reassuring tone when you talk to yourself. Say to yourself, "If I do everything just right, I'll make the basket." Bring your focus down to a fine, sharp point. Don't look around the gym, up in the crowd, or at the scoreboard. And don't stare at the hoop until you're ready to shoot.

With the negative thoughts eliminated from your mind, take a deep breath, and begin your mantra. *Feet square to the line. Bounce the ball three times, inflation hole up. Thumb in the channel. Elbow in. Bend the knees. Eye on the target. Shoot and follow through.* Let these familiar words, which have worked for you in the past, work in this situation, too.

DIVAC'S COMEBACK

Since I started this chapter with a negative scenario, I'd like to close with a positive one. Although Divac was devastated by his missed free throws in the playoffs, he worked hard to improve his free throw shooting, hoping he would have another chance to prove himself. It came on January 9, 1996, when the Lakers battled Minnesota. This time, Divac connected from the line with 12.2 seconds remaining and the Lakers claimed a 106–104 victory. Three nights later he made 12 of 15 free throws, including one with thirty-eight seconds left, which became the winning point.

"Now, when I go on the court, I feel so good," Divac was quoted as saying in the *Los Angeles Times*. "I feel powerful, like nobody can stop me. I want to go to the basket and force the team to foul me. Then they're going to put me on the line and I'm going to make it."

Divac has realized what every good player eventually understands: Every game, and every free throw, is a new opportunity to show that you're a winner.

7

Goal Setting for Improvement

> *Why not become at least a 70 percent free throw shooter? In what other sport can you pad your scoring average that way? I mean, after a penalty, [Florida quarterback] Danny Wuerffel doesn't get a free pass from the 50.*
>
> MIAMI HEAT SCOUT CHRIS WALLACE

Do you think you are capable of a 95 percent free throw average during this coming season? Did you laugh at that question and say, "No way"? Okay, what about a 90 percent free throw average? Well then, what about 85 percent? Or 80 percent? 75 percent?

Have you said, "Well, maybe . . ." yet? If you have, that's where your first goal should be. You should set your first goal just out of reach. It should be within the realm of possibility, but high enough so that the idea of achieving it really excites you. Your goal should excite you because, once you set it, there is an excellent chance you will reach it.

If high goals can be set and reached, why don't more players use them? Fear. Goals mean reaching outside of our comfort zone. Goals mean going against the advice we get from well-meaning advisors who caution, "Don't count your chickens before they hatch." Or peers who say, "What makes you so special?" Even parents who limit their children by saying, "If you expect too much you may be disappointed." I believe it is better to shoot high and be disappointed than to settle for mediocrity before the game even begins.

What makes goal setting so difficult is that, when it comes to assessing our own talents, we are too conservative. Let me give you an example.

COMPARISONS ARE DEADLY

When I played college ball, I remember how my teammates reacted when they walked out on the court before a big game. The first thing they did was check out the other team. "They're huge!" they'd say to each other. Or, "Look at that guy shoot! He's amazing!"

My teammates automatically inflated the other team's abilities—and reduced their own. Pretty soon we had fifteen psyched-out guys. The irony was that the other team was doing the same thing to us!

As an athlete, and throughout life, you should view your talents in the best light. Develop the habit of pushing yourself to achieve the highest level of which you are capable. Be proud of your accomplishments and take your disappointments in stride.

Above all else, don't measure yourself against your competition. If you do, you'll perform only well enough to beat them. Instead, dig down into yourself to find unused talents and reservoirs of energy. The best way to find out how good your really are is to set goals.

The topic of goal setting may bring a negative reaction. Young people tend to think of goal setting as a duty, something a parent, teacher or coach requires, but something that has no bearing on reality. But let me tell you, I've probably done a lot more living than you, and I have seen goals produce results that are almost magic. Goals work wonders.

As a basketball player you should probably have three goals. Have two goals pertaining to specific scoring averages and one for a character trait, like team leadership or motivation. But if you've never used goals before, why not start by setting a goal for free throw shooting? Set one goal for performance in practice and one for your game average. (It is usually thought that your average in practice will be about 5 percent higher than in games.) Once you see how well goal setting works for your free throw shooting, you won't have to be pushed into setting goals in the future.

HEAT-SEEKING MISSILE

I once heard a goal described as being like a heat-seeking missile. That's a vivid image that I think is accurate. It seeks and finds its target as if it had a mind of its own. Once you know where you are aiming, your subconscious "locks in" on the target with unshakable determination and doesn't quit until the job is done.

The beauty of goals is that they work for you during practice, in games and even while you sleep. That's because setting a goal is like dropping a powerful thought into the vast subconscious mind. The subconscious is the largest section of the mind. Yet we have only partial control over it. In the subconscious, the goal takes root, grows, and begins to manifest itself in a million small ways. What you've really done is boosted your self-image. You've told yourself you believe you are capable of a higher level of performance.

MY FIRST GOAL

As I mentioned earlier, I took up free throw shooting for something to do. Of course, I wanted to see improvement. My first goal, shooting 10 in a row, came quickly. The next hurdle—25 consecutive free throws—took much longer. I worked on that for months before I succeeded. Then I trained my sights on shooting 50 in a row, then 100.

Each time I set a new goal, I realized I was, in a sense, creating a new obstacle for myself. When trying to shoot 10 in a row, the last one was tough because so much was riding on it. Later, when shooting for 25, that tenth basket was nothing, while the twenty-fifth basket was difficult. I had to remind myself that these numbers were only obstacles *in my mind*. And I knew I could overcome them in my mind, as well. I soon saw that as my goals increased, past obstacles were forgotten and new ones appeared.

Whenever I faced an obstacle, I had to remind myself that one free throw is *exactly* like the next, whether it is the first, the ninth, or the twenty-fifth. Every free throw is alike whether it is being shot in an empty gym or in front of a cheering crowd of thousands. So I refused to let these obstacles take root in my mind. In time, I learned that overcoming obstacles made them gradually diminish and disappear.

As my free throw average increased and I extended my streak, I realized I needed a new goal—and one that was not just a higher number. One day, I heard on the radio that there were nine million American men my age. I remember thinking, "I'd like to be one of the ten best seventy-year-old free throw shooters in the country." This was the first step in setting the ultimate goal—to try to break the world's record. There was something intimidating about admitting, even to myself, that I wanted to achieve this distinction. I had to push aside all the so-called conventional wisdom that said I was too old, that I was too weak, or lacked the stamina or ability to concentrate that long.

Once the record was set, I realized that I had broken a barrier, not just for myself, but for people of all ages. I can't tell you how often high school players say to me, "If you can do it at your age, I know I can do it, too." Seeing one person set a record lifts up other people around them.

I laugh now at my early goals, and my struggle to achieve them, because I have exceeded them all by so much. But all those goals were important to my progress. If I had set my sights too high, too soon, I may have become discouraged and quit. Instead, my short-term goals were like rungs on a ladder, taking me to new heights, one step at a time.

SUCCESS IN ANY FORM

A strange and wonderful thing about goals is that they will always accomplish something good, even if it's not what the person had in mind when setting them.

My own story is an amazing example of this. When I was a teenager, I wanted to be a basketball star. I was working toward that goal when World War II broke out. My best years as an athlete were spent in the U.S. Navy, thousands of miles from the nearest basketball court. But that goal never completely died. Now, at the age of seventy-three, I'm more famous for shooting free throws than I would have been as one of three hundred pro basketball players. Besides that, free throw shooting has kept me out of trouble in my retirement years.

Keep this in mind as you set your goal. You can't control every detail of the future. Set specific goals, then let them surprise you with the form they take. The point is, setting goals will always bring you something good, even if it's not what you think you want right now.

BLUE SKYING

As you ponder the exact free throw average to shoot for, let me return to the question I asked at the beginning of the chapter: What is the very highest level of performance you are capable of? I'm not asking how well you *have* played. Or how well you might play by some fluke. I'm asking what you are capable of on the very best day of your life. Think about that deeply for a minute. I'll bet you anything your answer is way too low. The sad truth is that most of us grossly underestimate our abilities. In fact, I heard an expert on goal setting once offer this piece of advice: Make a realistic estimate of your talents, then add 10 percent.

As you set your goals, use the "blue sky" principle. I've heard this applied in business, but I think it works for athletics, too. Start by thinking of what you would want to accomplish in a perfect world. Don't think about yourself and your limitations—go for it! Pull your dreams out of the blue sky.

Now, if that's where you really want to go, then work backward. What are the steps you can take to lead you from here to there? And what are the goals you need to get you there?

A CONTRACT WITH YOURSELF

Now here's the hard part. I want you to write your goal on a three-by-five index card. Include a time span during which you plan to achieve your goal. If this is the beginning of the basketball season, set a goal for the season. If this is the off-season, set a goal to reach before practice starts.

A free throw goal is valuable because it is specific and measurable. True, it is only one aspect of your total performance as a basketball player. But it is an important one.

Improve at free throw shooting and the level of your entire game will rise.

After you've written out your goal, sign it. Then, put it someplace where you will see it periodically. Remind yourself what you are shooting for. You should even imagine yourself, in the future, looking at the card *after* you've achieved the goal. Imagine the pride you feel at your accomplishment.

Earlier in this book I said something that I have to repeat. It is what goal setting is all about: "We are more limited by our beliefs than our abilities." If you believe you are an average basketball player, you'll play like one. Believe you are a champion, and you'll eventually be one. Set your goals high and let them lift you up to where you really want to go.

8

Questions and Answers

David Letterman: How long did it take you [to set the record]?
Dr. Amberry: Twelve hours.
David Letterman: And why did you finally stop?
Dr. Amberry: They kicked me out of the gym.

Wherever I go, people ask me questions about my free throw shooting method and how I set the world's record. The most common question comes from kids. When they hear it took me twelve hours to shoot 2,750 consecutive free throws, they always ask, "Didn't you have to go to the bathroom?" Yes, I did take short breaks for that reason, and to have a light snack before I continued shooting.

In the rest of this chapter I'm going to answer some of the other questions I'm frequently asked. If you have a question, I hope it is on the list that I am including here.

Can you shoot blindfolded?

Players don't shoot free throws in games with blindfolds on. So I don't do it in practice. I'm not a trick shot artist.

While I have said many times that you don't need to stare at the basket, you do need to see it, at least for a split second before you shoot. Using your eyes correctly is an important part of the process.

How do you suggest warming up your free throw shot before a game?

Warming up your free throw is an important part of your warm-up routine. Before you shoot from the line, slowly back up, shooting the ball with the same elbow-in delivery. Build your confidence by seeing the ball go in the net several times before you attempt an actual free throw.

Once you are on the line, shoot a few free throws. Use this time to remind yourself of the seven steps. If you make, say, your first three free throws, leave it at that. If you miss one or two, shoot until you make maybe three in a row. The point is to stop practicing while you're on a streak. Tell yourself you've got the feel for the line and you're ready when the time comes.

If you are fouled early in the game, be eager to go to the line. In fact, some players try to draw a foul in the opening minutes of the game so they can shoot some free throws without end-game pressure. This builds confidence in their free throw, and it also puts them on the scoreboard with a couple of baskets. Every time you hit your free throws, let this keep your confidence factor high. Tell yourself the more free throws you make, the better the chances are of making your next free throws.

Is it true that it's harder for very tall players, like Wilt Chamberlain, to make their free throws?

That is one of many myths about free throw shooting. I think there were two factors that made Chamberlain a poor free throw shooter.

He wrote in his autobiography that he was an excellent

free throw shooter in high school. But later, he injured his knee so that when he bent it a certain way—the way he bent it at the free throw line—it hurt him. This actually supports my belief that the legs are an important part of free throw shooting. Without good knee bend, Chamberlain may have been trying to shoot only with his arm. His distance control and accuracy would suffer as a result.

The other thing that hurt Wilt Chamberlain was the negative publicity his poor free throw shooting brought him. With any great player the press tries to find some weak area to publicize. Free throw shooting was his weakness—although he was outstanding in every other way. Sportswriters continually questioned him about his free throw shooting and eventually it became a mental obstacle that he couldn't overcome.

There may be some truth to the fact that very tall players have a harder time preventing unnecessary motion which could conceivably throw off their accuracy. However, for every Wilt Chamberlain who can't shoot free throws, there are many examples of very tall players who are strong at the line.

I've heard it said that your free throw shooting skill stems from the fact that you have very large hands. Is this true?

First of all, my hands aren't large. In fact, they are probably small for a person of my height—6'7". Furthermore, I don't believe that the size of a person's hands has any bearing on his or her ability to shoot free throws. Anyone with normal sized hands can be a great free throw shooter.

Canards like this, and the one about tall players having difficulty at the line, are probably started by lazy players.

They are looking at an excuse to explain their own poor performance at free throw shooting. The simple truth is, if you use good mechanics, practice regularly, and are in control of your thoughts, you will be a good free throw shooter.

Bringing my elbow in feels really awkward. Besides, I shoot from the perimeter with my elbow out. Do I really have to do it?

I'm not asking you to change your whole style of shooting. If you want to shoot from the outside with your elbow stuck out, that's up to you. Many good players do the same thing and are successful with it. Usually, a player sticks his or her elbow out to keep defenders away. But remember, free throws are different. No one's in your face. There is no reason to have your elbow out. And doing so will hurt the accuracy of the shot.

Besides, it makes good sense to keep your elbow tucked in. Right now, wherever you are, pretend you're holding a basketball. Place your elbow as close to your navel as you can. Now straighten your arm. It naturally goes toward an imaginary basket. Try the same thing with your elbow out. As your arm straightens, it moves *across* the basket. This shows how easy it is to miss the basket to the right or left.

I'm a good shooter. I don't see why I can't just go up there and shoot my free throws just like a jumper.

This is what many players do—even NBA stars. And I think this is where most players go wrong. They fail to recognize that the free throw is a unique shot, with specific demands and requirements.

As I said earlier, the free throw bears closest resemblance to a set shot—as old-fashioned as that may seem.

In the old days, when a player was undefended near the basket, he would stop, plant his feet, and take a set shot. It was the most accurate way of shooting a basket.

As defenders became larger and more aggressive, players got used to shooting the jumper to beat their man by going up and over. The set shot was slowly forgotten. And the free throw average of modern players began to slip. This was because they didn't use a set shot from the line.

I feel that my high free throw average, 98 percent, proves that my method is the best to use under pressure. Who cares if the set shot is old-fashioned? What people will remember most is who won the game.

What do you know about pressure? You're not playing basketball now. You don't shoot your free throws under game conditions.

The person with the most to lose is under the greatest pressure. Right now, I'm the world's greatest free throw shooter. If someone challenges me and I lose, I've lost the world's championship.

It's true. I'm not under the same kind of pressure NBA players are, but I'm under pressure nonetheless. When I shot free throws on *Letterman,* they told me I had to make my first two free throws. They didn't even give me the six seconds I usually take. (In a game you get ten seconds to shoot each free throw.) I had a different earphone in each ear. When the director cut to me the producer yelled, "Shoot! Shoot!" And I made both free throws.

People also say to me, "The pros shoot their free throws at the end of the game when they're exhausted. You're not tired when you shoot yours." It took me twelve hours to set the world's record. I can tell you, after eleven hours on my feet, I was exhausted. And I was seventy-one years old at the time.

Should you keep your head still when you shoot free throws?

This is probably the most often cited rule in golf instruction. And now it is finding its way into free throw shooting. This may stem from the fact that golf is the favorite second sport of many basketball players, including Michael Jordan.

In golf, keeping your head still is important because the head is the "hub" of the swing. Your body turns around your head. You don't want to sway back and forth. However, there are those golfers who feel that concentrating on keeping the head still creates rigidity throughout your body.

Yes, it's important to eliminate unnecessary motion when shooting free throws. But I live by the KISS rule—"Keep It Simple (Stupid)." I don't want to give players anything more to think about. Besides that, there is already enough tension at the free throw line. Instead of trying to freeze your head in one place, concentrate on making your movements relaxed and smooth.

My coach tells me to be ready to follow my free throw. If I miss, I might get the rebound. Do you agree with this strategy?

You also hear coaches say to shoot free throws with a very high arc. If the shot misses, the rebound will be easier. With all due respect to your coach, and coaches everywhere who think this works, you should never anticipate a miss. This undermines your mental game. On the free throw line you have to be completely convinced you are going to make the shot.

If shooting 100 free throws a day is good, is shooting 200 even better?

Yes. If you have the time to shoot that many, by all means do it. The extra practice will push you to an even higher free throw percentage and possibly bring you attention from your coach and the fans. It's also important to remember that when you're practicing free throws, you are also reinforcing good shooting fundamentals. So free throw practice is doing double duty.

I shoot 500 free throws a day. That's because my goal is to be a 100 percent free throw shooter. I'm actually at about 98 percent.

Free throw shooting skills need to be practiced and maintained constantly to keep them sharp. It takes time, but when you are under pressure and need to sink a clutch basket, every minute of practice you spent will be worth it.

Your seven steps are a lot to remember. Do you really have to do them all just to make one basket?

You should be glad it's a lot to remember—it will take your mind off the pressure you're facing at the free throw line. Every step is important. But that's not to say that if one step is done incorrectly, your body won't sense this and compensate later. Remember to focus on the process, not the results. If the process is done correctly, the result will take care of itself.

With a little practice you will find that the physical steps are easy to remember. In one or two practice sessions you can blend them and make them automatic. The mental steps then become most important. Find the inflation hole, let it center you, and remove doubt before you shoot with the image of the 15-foot-long arm.

Can a higher free throw average help my shooting from the floor?

From the coaches I've talked to, there seems to be a strong connection between free throw shooting and three-pointers. There are two reasons for this. The first is mechanics, the second is confidence.

Many shooting coaches advocate squaring up to the basket *even when you're shooting your jumpers*. My method is to put your feet square to the line. This is good training for your outside shots. As you see your free throw average climb, you are subconsciously going to imitate its success in other areas of your game.

Confidence has been described as the most important element of success in any sport. When you sink a basket, your confidence increases—whether it's a free throw or a layup. When you make your free throws, you're showing the other team that your game is complete. They can foul you if they want, but it's going to cost them two points. The more free throws you make, the more your game level will climb.

You've said, "We are more limited by our beliefs than our abilities." What do you mean by that?

The term "gifted athlete" has created unrealistic expectations. There is a popular misconception that your athletic ability is set at birth—you are given a certain amount of skill, and there is little that can be done to change that.

On the contrary, many of the greatest athletes had to work hard, both mentally and physically, to succeed. Ben Hogan, the famous golfer, was critically injured in an auto accident when he was at the peak of his career. He was told he would never walk again. Not only did he teach himself to walk again, but he returned to professional golf and won many major championships.

Ultimately, the mental game is where we can make the greatest gains. If you think of yourself as a loser or a choke artist, you will probably become one. But if you think of yourself as a champion—and you learn the mechanics of your game and practice hard—eventually you will play like one.

INDEX

Dr. Tom Amberry was a podiatrist for 40 years, publishing many articles about various aspects of his profession. On November 15, 1993, following his retirement, Dr. Amberry shot his way into *The Guinness Book of Records* by sinking 2,750 free throws in a row. Since then he has become internationally known as, in the words of one announcer, "the best free throw shooter ever to touch a basketball." Dr. Amberry travels constantly, teaches shooting clinics and makes frequent radio and TV appearances. He has been featured on *NBC Nightly News with Tom Brokaw*, ESPN, *Dateline, Day One, The Late Show with David Letterman, NBA Inside Stuff*, and ABCs *World News Tonight*. On his college basketball team, Tom Amberry was twice the nation's high scorer. He was an All-American two years in a row, turning down a two-year, no-cut contract with the Lakers to pursue a career in medicine.

Philip Reed combines his two greatest passions in *Free Throw*: sports and writing. He has been fascinated with many different sports and has played on baseball, basketball, tennis, lacrosse, and soccer teams. He was a reporter for *The Rocky Mountain News* in Denver, his screenplays have been produced for network television, and his plays have been staged in Los Angeles, San Francisco, Chicago, and New York. He is the author of five other non-fiction books and a novel, *Bird Dog*.